CATALYZE:

The Rise of LGBTQ+ Movements in the Middle East & North Africa

About the Author

Mike Figueredo obtained his Bachelor's and Master's in Political Science from the Mark O. Hatfield School of Government at Portland State University. His focus of study was electoral engineering and social movements within the subfield of comparative politics. He temporarily pursued his Doctorate in Politics & Public Policy at the same institution, but left that program to host *The Humanist Report* full-time. *The Humanist Report* has amassed nearly half a million YouTube subscribers and more than 150 million views. Mike has advocated for a plethora of political issues during his time hosting *The Humanist Report*, but rose to prominence primarily over his coverage of the 2016 and 2020 elections and for his championing of net neutrality, single-payer healthcare, and LGBTQ+ rights. Aside from his advocacy Mike is a self-proclaimed nerd, video game enthusiast and dog lover.

Dedication

I dedicate this book to all of my wonderful viewers as well as every LGBTQ+ person fighting for equality around the world. Social justice activists in socially conservative authoritarian regimes *do* exist. If you're a queer person in these states who feels trapped, unseen, and hopeless, please know that there are people that care deeply about your righteous cause. We see you. You are valid. You are worthy. I dedicate this book to each and every one of you. I also dedicate this book to the resilient Palestinians living in Gaza, who are facing an ethnic cleansing and genocide at the hands of the Israeli government with the full backing of the United States. This gut-wrenching siege is taking place at the very moment I write this. As human beings we all have a moral obligation to condemn these unfathomable atrocities and elevate the voices of the Palestinian people wherever we can.

Table of Contents

Chapter 7
Conclusion & Implications for Social Movement Research
148

PREFACE

A Time of Uncertainty for LGBTQ+ People

The 2010s, generally speaking, ushered in progress and heightened visibility for queer people, especially in the United States. The discriminatory Clinton-era military policy of 'Don't Ask Don't Tell' (DADT) was repealed, same-sex couples won equal marriage rights at the U.S. Supreme Court, public opinion shifted favorably towards gay rights, and trans visibility reached an all-time high with trans stories being shared in television series such as *Orange is the New Black, Glee* and *Transparent*. However, the pendulum begun to swing in the opposite direction towards the end of the decade after Republican politicians opted to end their tactical retreat[1] on LGBTQ+ issues. While the Republican Party may have been pressured to de-emphasize their

---

[1] This was a term used by *Slate's* Mark Joseph Stern to describe the Republican Party's resuscitation of "the kind of casual homophobia that seemed to be waning" in a tweet on March 30, 2022 about backlash to gay fathers. It can be viewed here: https://twitter.com/mjs_DC/status/1509192726021132291.

opposition to queer civil rights after their explicit homophobia became a political liability, the Party never fully dropped their opposition to LGBTQ+ rights; but rather, switched to different targets within the community in lieu of surrendering on the issue altogether. Much of the same rhetoric, stereotypes, and political tactics used against gay men and women in the '90s and '00s were recycled for transphobic purposes in the late '10s, as "gender ideology" overtook "sexual deviancy" as the GOP's new boogeyman in the Trump-era.

President Trump reversed Obama-era protections for trans students, unilaterally enacted his own version of DADT by banning transgender Americans from serving in the military, and his Justice Department announced they would "no longer argue in court that transgender people are federally protected from employment discrimination"[2] in his first year in office. While Trump implemented new transphobic policies at the onset of his term, his administration remained ostensibly supportive of gays, lesbians and bisexuals. For example, Richard Grenell, an openly gay man who served as U.S. ambassador to Germany under the Trump administration, led a global initiative to decriminalize homosexuality around the globe; although Trump was seemingly unaware of his own administration's effort to do this and "seemed

---

[2] Selena Simmons-Duffin, "'Whiplash' Of LGBTQ Protections And Rights, From Obama To Trump," *NPR*, last modified March 2, 2020, accessed, https://www.npr.org/sections/health-shots/2020/03/02/804873211/whiplash-of-lgbtq-protections-and-rights-from-obama-to-trump

genuinely confused"3 when asked about it by reporters. More importantly, his judicial appointments were Federalist Society evangelicals with originalist interpretations of the U.S. Constitution, meaning their views towards sexual and gender minorities were *very* negative to put it mildly. This mattered for the fact that LGBTQ+ people fought and won many rights through the U.S. court system, and Trump's socially conservative judicial appointments made that avenue less workable for LGBTQ+ people looking to expand their rights. Trump's appointments signaled the beginning of a shift in momentum against queer rights even though he wasn't *as* explicitly hostile towards queer people (excluding trans and non-binary Americans) as his Republican predecessors. Nevertheless, Trump was ambivalent (at best) towards gay rights.

After Trump's term ended in a failed attempt to overturn the 2020 election, Republican politicians and voters seemed politically aimless—at least rhetorically—and became obsessed with esoteric philosophies like critical race theory as well as buzzwords like "woke" and "cancel culture." They also developed an affinity for conspiracy theories about the aforementioned election and the COVID vaccine; that is, until social conservatives took the reins and set an agenda they could all get behind. Social conservatives successfully elevated the salience of trans issues and reestablished bigotry as their de facto agenda by 2022. Trans people were designated as the common enemy the Party could

---

3 Steve Benen, "Trump seems unaware of his plan to end criminalization of homosexuality," *NBC News*, last modified February 21, 2019, accessed March 3, 2024, https://www.msnbc.com/rachel-maddow-show/trump-seems-unaware-his-plan-end-criminalization-homosexuality-msna1197141

collectively unite against. That opposition has remained constant (more or less) ever since. The reanimation of anti-LGBTQ+ hardliners hasn't necessarily yielded much electoral success for Republicans in 2022 and 2023[4] at the national level; but they've remained steadfast and undeterred, and have managed to make *significant* gains in some states. Florida and Texas have lead the charge in reversing queer rights and protections (especially for trans and non-binary people). Consequently, many of the remaining wins made by queer activists in the 2010s have either been eliminated or placed on the chopping block, and new ways to criminalize and police the existence of sexual and gender minorities are being devised regularly.

Conservative Supreme Court justices Clarence Thomas and Samuel Alito have openly signaled their desire to overturn the Court's landmark 2015 decision *Obergefell v. Hodges*, which struck down bans on same-sex marriages. In *303 Creative LLC v. Elenis* the conservative supermajority on the Supreme Court gave anti-LGBTQ+ business owners what Justice Sotomayor called a "license to discriminate" against queer people under the guise of free speech.[5]

Additionally, Republicans in state legislatures across the country have waged an all-out war on trans existence; bathroom usage of trans people has been legislated by some states, trans

---

[4] Christopher Wilson, "2023 election results: Anti-trans attacks continue to lose in swing races," *Yahoo! News*, last modified November 8, 2023, accessed March 4, 2024, https://news.yahoo.com/2023-election-anti-trans-attacks-fail-kentucky-governor-beshear-loudon-bucks-school-boards-danica-roem-155825340.html

[5] Andrew Chung, "US Supreme Court deals blow to LGBT rights in web designer case," *Reuters*, last modified June 30, 2023, accessed March 3, 2024, https://www.reuters.com/legal/us-supreme-court-rule-web-designer-with-anti-gay-marriage-stance-2023-06-30/

athletes have been banned from all kinds of sports (including non-physical sports like chess),[6] and access to gender-affirming care has been restricted or banned for minors (and even adults in some states). A Data For Progress poll finds that 38% of transgender adults are considering leaving their state in response to anti-trans policies.[7] Results from a survey conducted by the National Center for Transgender Equality of 92,000 transgender and non-binary respondents are even more alarming: around 4,500 trans Americans have *already* fled their state and 47% considered leaving.[8]

The Right-Wing War on Queer People

The climate around queer issues has become alarmingly toxic in this era. Right-wing political commentators have

---

[6] Jamey Keaten, "The world's top chess federation won't let transgender women compete until 'relevant proof' is accepted by officials," *Fortune*, last modified August 21, 2023, accessed March 3, 2024, https://fortune.com/europe/2023/08/21/transgender-women-chess-competitions-fide-federation-switzerland/#:~:text=The%20world%27s%20top%20chess%20federation%20has%20ruled%20that%20transgender%20women,an%20assessment%20of%20gender%20change

[7] Kirby Phares, Rob Todaro, Grace Adcox, and Abby Springs, "Anti-LGBTQ+ Policies and Rhetoric Are Harming LGBTQ+ Lives," *Data For Progress*, last modified March 2024, accessed March 29, 2024, https://www.filesforprogress.org/memos/Anti-LGBTQ-Policies-and-Rhetoric-Are-Harming-LGBTQ-Lives.pdf

[8] Brooke Migdon, "Half of trans people in US have considered moving out of state. Because of anti-LGBTQ laws: Survey," *The Hill*, last modified February 7, 2024, accessed February 25, 2024, https://thehill.com/policy/healthcare/4452248-half-of-trans-people-in-us-have-considered-moving-out-of-state-because-of-anti-lgbtq-laws-survey/

espoused cruel and downright genocidal rhetoric about trans Americans. Notably, far right christian nationalist ideologue Michael Knowles called for "transgenderism" to be eradicated at the March 2023 CPAC conference to applause from the audience.[9] At the following CPAC Knowles called marriage "the union of a man and woman" during an anti-same-sex marriage screed.[10] Singer Kid Rock spearheaded a months-long boycott against Bud Light by shooting cases of beer in a viral video in response to the company's sponsored social media post with Dylan Mulvaney, a trans influencer. She later revealed that she was inundated with harassment and death threats as a result. Stochastic terrorism towards LGBTQ+ people—disproportionately aimed at trans and non-binary people—in that same year was correlated with an "epidemic of violence" according to the Human Rights Campaign following the murder of 33 trans and non-binary Americans.[11]

Predictably, hysteria towards trans Americans soon extended to the rest of the LGBTQ+ community. Old homophobic tropes about homosexual men being sexual predators that pose a danger to children were brought back from the dead. The

---

[9] Patrick Reis, "CPAC Speaker Calls for Eradication of 'Transgenderism' — and Somehow Claims He's Not Calling for Elimination of Transgender People," *Rolling Stone*, last modified March 6, 2023, accessed February 25, 2024, https://www.rollingstone.com/politics/politics-news/cpac-speaker-transgender-people-eradicated-1234690924/

[10] A video of Knowles' speech was shared on X (formerly Twitter) by the @BidenHQ account here: https://x.com/BidenHQ/status/1760804455283298476?s=20

[11] Brooke Migdon, "'Epidemic of violence' targets transgender community, with at least 33 deaths cited in report," *The Hill*, last modified November 20, 2023, accessed February 25, 2024, https://thehill.com/homenews/lgbtq/4319195-transgender-epidemic-violence-hrc-report/

accusation of "grooming" has been lobbed at so many queer people (without evidence) that the word "groomer" itself has become a common anti-gay slur used by conservatives to attack *all* queer people and their allies. It has been suggested that the mere *representation* of queer people in society is tantamount to "grooming" of children; with the assumption being that LGBTQ+ people can "groom" children to adopt a queer orientation or trans identity by simply being in their presence. This homophobic and transphobic rhetoric has been parroted everywhere, including on Spotify's *The Joe Rogan Experience*, which is the largest podcast in the world.

Openly gay conservative commentator Dave Rubin—who tried to ingratiate himself with his right-wing colleagues by attacking trans people—was inundated with ridicule following the announcement that he and his husband were having children via a surrogate. Milo Yiannapoulous, who purports to be "ex-gay," publicly remarked that Rubin should be executed in response to the announcement. Ironically, Rubin still parrots right-wing talking points about movies "grooming" kids by simply featuring LGBTQ+ characters. Other high-profile gay couples were attacked for simply having children, including YouTuber Shane Dawson and his husband as well as U.S. Transportation Secretary Pete Buttigieg and his husband.

But gay adoption and surrogacy wasn't the only gay rights issue with a renewed focus. Perhaps for the first time in decades drag queens became the focus of social conservatives following an astroturfed fear-mongering campaign spearheaded, in part, by right-wing stochastic terrorists like Chaya Raichik of the notoriously popular 'Libs of TikTok' account on X (formerly known as Twitter). David Ingram of NBC News reports that anti-LGBTQ+ social media posts by Libs of TikTok resulted in "at least 21 bomb threats."[12] Retailers like Target—a long-time ostensible ally to the LGBTQ+ community—announced in 2023 its decision to remove pride displays following vandalism and harassment of its employees by anti-LGBTQ+ zealots.[13] Predictably, hate-motivated crimes against LGBTQ+ people have been on the rise too. 28-year-old O'Shae Sibley, a professional dancer and openly gay man, was stabbed to death at a gas station in Brooklyn "because he was gay" according to his friend.[14] Sibley and his friends were "voguing and dancing" while pumping their gas when a homophobic group harassed them and reportedly called them homophobic slurs before committing the hate crime against him.

Overall, there were more than 700 incidents of anti-LGBTQ+ violence ranging from harassment to murder according to a joint report by several organizations.[15] After a 2022 mass

---

[12] David Ingram, "After Libs of TikTok posted, at least 21 bomb threats followed," *NBC News*, last modified February 7, 2024, accessed February 25, 2024, https://www.nbcnews.com/tech/internet/libs-tiktok-x-chaya-raichik-bomb-threat-twitter-of-libsoftiktok-rcna102784

[13] Graeme Massie, "Trans couple harassed in Montana Target by man throwing Pride clothes on floor," Independent, last modified May 30, 2023, accessed February 25, 2024, https://www.independent.co.uk/news/world/americas/target-montana-trans-couple-pride-b2347906.html

[14] Kiara Alfonseca, "Deadly stabbing of gay man at NYC gas station investigated as potential hate crime," *ABC News*, last modified August 1, 2023, accessed February 25, 2024, https://abcnews.go.com/US/deadly-stabbing-gay-man-nyc-gas-station-investigated/story?id=101895258

[15] Brooke Migdon, "LGBTQ people targeted in more than 700 incidents since last year: Report," *The Hill*, last modified November 16, 2023, accessed February 25, 2024, https://thehill.com/homenews/lgbtq/4313588-lgbtq-people-targeted-700-incidents-2023-report/

shooting at a drag show hosted by Club Q in Colorado left five dead, prominent conservatives such as Tucker Carlson and Tim Pool justified the shooter's killing spree.[16] On his Fox News program Tucker Carlson's chyron read "STOP SEXUALIZING KIDS" in reference to kid-friendly drag shows. Tim Pool wrote on X (formerly Twitter) that Club Q hosted a "grooming event" and that society "shouldn't tolerate pedophiles grooming kids."[17] There was no evidence of "grooming" or pedophilia taking place at Club Q, however, conservatives often erroneously (and purposefully) equate age-appropriate drag shows and pride events with sexual grooming in an effort to make Americans suspicious of queer people. But the expression of violent sentiments towards LGBTQ+ people—while common and alarming—isn't yet as ubiquitous as more casual, ignorant bigotry towards queer people by conservatives and non-conservatives alike.

Unreliable Support from Ambivalent Liberal Allies

Comedians such as Dave Chappelle and Ricky Gervais as well as *Harry Potter* author J.K. Rowling have adopted right-wing arguments against trans Americans in particular. That general skepticism towards trans people, in many cases, has morphed into outright hostility. J.K. Rowling, for example, initially only dabbled in transphobia by raising concerns about trans women in

---

[16] Ben Goggin and Kat Tenbarge, "Right-wing influencers and media double down on anti-LGBTQ rhetoric in the wake of the Colorado shooting," *NBC News*, last modified November 23, 2022, accessed February 25, 2024, https://www.nbcnews.com/tech/internet/right-wing-influencers-media-double-anti-lgbtq-rhetoric-wake-colorado-rcna58371

[17] See citation in previous footnote.

spaces traditionally reserved for cis women. She's now explicitly hostile towards trans people and openly associates with the bigoted TERF (Trans-Exclusionary Radical Feminist) movement and has even purposefully misgendered trans people. On X (formerly Twitter), Rowling called a trans woman a "man" that was "cosplaying" as a woman,[18] cited faulty "evidence" from Dr. David Bell[19] (an anti-LGBTQ+ charlatan who promotes conversion therapy), and even arguably engaged in holocaust denial by rejecting the fact that Nazis burned research from Magnus Hirschfeld, who was at the forefront of gender and sexuality research at the time.[20] Although Rowling's obsessive tweets about her grievances with trans people has sparked social backlash, her bigotry hasn't yet cost her monetarily; and while she's likely lost a lot of fans over her transphobia, it's helped her form new friendships with like-minded celebrity bigots. Dave Chappelle, for example, infamously defended her in a comedy special and declared himself to be on "team TERF," then subsequently doubled-down on transphobia after his comedy

---

[18] Erin Reed, "JK Rowling Transphobia: Rowling Calls Trans Woman Journalist 'A Man…Cosplaying'," *Erin in the Morning*, last modified March 4, 2024, accessed March 4, 2024, https://www.erininthemorning.com/p/jk-rowling-transphobia-rowling-calls

[19] J.K. Rowling, X (formerly Twitter), *@jk_rowling*, posted March 12, 2024, accessed March 13, 2024, https://x.com/jk_rowling/status/1767641731397214517?s=20

[20] The Serfs, X (formerly Twitter), *@theserfstv*, posted March 13, 2024, accessed March 13, 2024, https://x.com/theserfstv/status/1767965104900067695?s=20

special sparked immense backlash.[21] In his next comedy special he not only doubled down on transphobia, but took shots at other members of the LGBTQ+ community with a homophobic quip about rapper Lil Nas X that insinuated he was trying to flaunt his sexuality "at 10 o'clock on BET while all the kids are awake and can see" him,[22] which played directly into the right's fear mongering about so-called gay "groomers." Since the underlying bias towards gay and trans people is fundamentally the same,[23] it's almost inevitable to see one's transphobia morph into homophobia or vice versa. But authors and comedians haven't been the only celebrities taking aim at trans people.

Liberal intellectuals that have been generally supportive of LGBTQ+ people such as Richard Dawkins has been so overtly bigoted towards trans people his 'humanist of the year' awards were withdrawn by the American Humanist Association.[24]

---

[21] Zoe Christen Jones, "Netflix employees stage walkout over Dave Chappelle special," *CBS News*, last modified October 25, 2021, accessed February 25, 2024, https://www.cbsnews.com/news/dave-chappelle-netflix-employees-walkout/

[22] Alexander Del Rosario, "Lil Nas X saw Dave Chappelle's 'Dreamer' dig, and he threw shade right back," *Los Angeles Times*, last modified January 4, 2024, accessed Mach 3, 2024, https://www.latimes.com/entertainment-arts/music/story/2024-01-04/lil-nas-x-dave-chappelle-the-dreamer-netflix-special

[23] The bias referred to is a violation of societal gender norms. All members of the LGBTQ+ community violate gender expectations in some way, shape or form; and that deviation from ascribed gender norms is the basis of discrimination against them.

[24] Alison Flood, "Richard Dawkins loses 'humanist of the year' title over trans comments," *The Guardian*, last modified April 20, 2021, accessed February 25, 2024, https://www.theguardian.com/books/2021/apr/20/richard-dawkins-loses-humanist-of-the-year-trans-comments

Furthermore, progressive news outlet *The Young Turks*' executive producer Ana Kasparian—a longtime ally to the LGBTQ+ community—inexplicably condemned use of the term "birthing person" (which is used in medical and legal settings to objectively categorize trans men and non-binary people who have the capacity to get pregnant)[25] despite the fact that she passionately defended inclusive language for pregnant trans people less than a year earlier.[26] Kasparian was confronted by her peers about the dangers of her rhetoric and how anti-trans conservatives would inevitably use her denunciation of inclusive language as much-needed liberal validation that their bias and bigotry against trans people was justified. Sure enough, anti-trans conservatives made an example out of the Kasparian kerfuffle and interpreted her denunciation as vindication. An article in Fox News reported on the liberal "melt down" in response to Kasparian's comments, with yours truly being quoted in the article as one of the "liberals" supposedly melting down.[27] Kristine Parks of Fox News wrote: "Mike Figueredo, host of a leftist political news show, claimed Kasparian was using a play 'right out of the right's anti-trans 'war on women'

---

[25] Kristine Parks and Jessica Chasmar, "Ana Kasparian doubles down after bashing trans-inclusive term 'birthing persons' as 'degrading' to women," *New York Post*, last modified April 12, 2023, accessed February 25, 2024, https://nypost.com/2023/04/12/ana-kasparian-doubles-down-bashing-birthing-person-language/

[26] Ana Kasparian and John Iadarola, "Prof. Khiara Bridges SHUTS DOWN Josh Hawley's Transphobic Questions During Congressional Hearing," *The Young Turks*, published July 13, 2022, accessed February 25, 2024, https://www.youtube.com/watch?v=LoElxFKjDoc

[27] Note: I'm not a liberal. Furthermore, my response to Kasparian (someone I considered a friend) was respectful.

playbook.'"[28] What could have been a good faith dialogue about allyship between like-minded peers devolved into sensationalist fodder for right-wing transphobes. Staunch conservatives like Kari Lake, Ian Miles Chong, Candace Owens and Ben Shapiro applauded Kasparian with praise and/or retweets.

But this was only the start of TYT's anti-trans trajectory. Kasparian and Cenk Uygur, the host and founder of TYT, later criticized the tactics used by trans rights activists during a protest of a speech by anti-trans provocateur Riley Gaines, and Uygur later vocalized opposition to trans women in sports at the collegiate level.[29] Kasparian continued to express skepticism about trans issues[30] and even defended anti-trans journalist Jesse Singal, who routinely exaggerates and sensationalizes stories of "de-transitioners" in an effort to drive skepticism about the efficacy of gender affirming care for minors. GLAAD reports, "Singal's story was cited in a legal brief filed by seven state attorneys general in a federal lawsuit seeking to roll back a trans

---

[28] Kristine Parks, "Liberals melt down after far-left journalist blasts 'birthing person' language: 'Oh f--- off'," *Fox News*, last modified March 23, 2023, accessed February 25, 2024, https://www.foxnews.com/media/liberals-melt-down-far-left-journalist-blasts-birthing-person-language-f-off

[29] Cenk Uygur and Ana Kasparian, "Trump Moans At Transgender Athletes in Women's Sports," *The Young Turks*, published on June 26, 2023, accessed February 25, 2024, https://www.youtube.com/watch?v=rjJz6rELHu4&t=0s

[30] "Talking to ANA KASPARIAN of THE YOUNG TURKS About Politics & Culture - Sitch & Adam Show 273," *Sitch & Adam Show*, published July 2, 2023, accessed February 25, 2024, https://www.youtube.com/watch?v=z8TD2jNPLK4

person's access to healthcare."[31] Singal's contribution to the anti-trans movement to ban gender-affirming healthcare has been widely known, but Kasparian defended him from accusations of transphobia and claimed she was a fan of his podcast.[32]

The abrupt shift in rhetoric from a network that calls itself the "home of progressives" lead to multiple LGBTQ+ people leaving TYT.[33] Before announcing her resignation, Bennie Carollo, a TYT contributor who's trans, says she offered to have an on-air conversation with Cenk Uygur about her issues with the channel's trans coverage for educational purposes.[34] Uygur never took her up on the offer despite his general inclination to debate disagreements with co-hosts and channel partners on-air. Uygur regularly platforms comedian Ben Gleib for heated debates, where

[31] "Jesse Singal," *GLAAD* (Gay & Lesbian Alliance Against Defamation), last modified April 21, 2023, accessed February 25, 2024, https://glaad.org/gap/jesse-singal/

[32] "Talking to ANA KASPARIAN of THE YOUNG TURKS About Politics & Culture - Sitch & Adam Show 273," *Sitch & Adam Show*, published July 2, 2023, accessed February 25, 2024, https://www.youtube.com/watch?v=z8TD2jNPLK4

[33] Mike Figueredo, "Trans TYT Employee Quits, Condemns Cenk Uygur & Ana Kasparian's Anti-Trans Rhetoric," *The Humanist Report*, published July 6, 2023, accessed February 25, 2024, https://youtu.be/Uk-O_PErl3w?si=bsTr6nE1WQ_krCro

[34] Bennie Carollo, "Why I left TYT," *Bennie Carollo*, published July 4, 2023, accessed February 25, 2024, https://youtu.be/_6DiIQWb0DE?si=7LvMqnTgJ1xdHdA6

Gleib defends Israel amid their siege on Gaza,[35] yet Uygur refused to engage with a trans employee about disagreements he dismissed as minor; worse yet, he publicly attacked Carollo and called her "unhinged" in a viral post to his 600,000+ followers on X (formerly Twitter).[36] This isn't surprising considering the fact that trans people rarely have the opportunity to defend and humanize themselves in the face of anti-trans bigotry, but it was particularly jarring for a progressive network that *should* know better to do the same. TYT's liberal hosts, however, aren't uniquely susceptible to anti-trans hysteria, and me seemingly belaboring this example about their shift serves as an important (and unfortunate) reminder that support from cis and straight allies is not unconditional and is very much subject to change, hence why social conservatives have been able to shift momentum back in their favor in the 2020s after substantial progress was made in the 2010s.

The Volatility of Support

The increasingly common phenomenon of straight, cis allies—who have historically been supportive of LGBTQ+ rights —being persuaded by transphobic talking points is one of many indications that the far right has gained significant ground in their culture war against trans Americans. Even liberals and

---

[35] Cenk Uygur, Ben Gleib and Mark Thompson, "Israel's Humanitarian Pause Leads to HEATED Debate Between TYT Hosts," *The Young Turks*, published November 10, 2023, accessed February 25, 2024, https://youtu.be/ EEsV_unSUNo?si=ULSYpI8-B5iiLMej

[36] Cenk Uygur, X (formerly Twitter), @cenkuygur, July 6, 2023, accessed February 25, 2024, https://twitter.com/cenkuygur/status/1677145391421337601

progressives have been relatively receptive to the bigoted arguments being used against queer people, including cis gays and lesbians. Elon Musk, the world's richest man, went from boasting about Tesla's perfect corporate equality score on June 1st of 2022[37] to promoting The Daily Wire's transphobic documentary *"What is a Woman?"* across his social media platform on June 2nd of 2023.[38] Sure, he's struggled to accept the gender identity of his estranged trans daughter[39] (which has, in turn, fueled his anger towards trans people more broadly), but one year is a *very* quick turnaround for such a drastic shift. But he's not alone in his sudden change of heart on issues pertaining to sexual and gender minorities. A poll conducted by Yahoo! News and YouGov found that just 52% of Democrats opposed Ron DeSantis' discriminatory 'Don't Say Gay' law,[40] which is uncharacteristic of a political group that has typically supported queer rights overwhelmingly. Moreover, a survey of 22,000 adults conducted by the Public Religion Research Institute found that support for same-sex marriage fell from its record high of 69% in 2022 to 67% the

---

[37] Elon Musk, X (formerly Twitter), @elonmusk, posted June 1, 2022, accessed February 25, 2024, https://twitter.com/elonmusk/status/1532030554778087424

[38] Elon Musk, X (formerly Twitter), @elonmusk, posted June 2, 2023, accessed February 25, 2024, https://twitter.com/elonmusk/status/1664609193230204929

[39] Danielle Campoamor, "Elon Musk blames school for rift with daughter: 'She doesn't want to spend time with me'," *Today*, last modified September 1, 2023, accessed February 25, 2024, https://www.today.com/parents/dads/elon-musk-daughter-school-biography-rcna103042

[40] Andrew Romano, "Poll: Only 52% of Democrats oppose Florida's 'Don't Say Gay' policy," *Yahoo! News*, last modified April 6, 2022, accessed February 25, 2024, https://news.yahoo.com/poll-only-52-of-democrats-oppose-floridas-dont-say-gay-policy-214144683.html

following year, with support from Democratic voters dropping from 83% to 82% and support from Republican voters declining from 49% to 47%.[41] After making significant strides in the 2010s, a potential swing among Democratic Party voters towards anti-LGBTQ+ politics is a reminder of how fickle people are on the issue of LGBTQ+ rights. They're generally supportive overall, but that support is *not* guaranteed in perpetuity.

In fact, many queer people encounter individuals that initially accept or reject them, but later have a change of heart. I've personally experienced rejection, then acceptance, then rejection again, then acceptance again just from one family member. Feelings of straight and cis people can be ambivalent; and consequently, support for their queer peers may oscillate between positive and negative depending on an increase in religiosity, new friends or romantic partners with hostile views towards queer people, or a change in political orientation that leads to the adoption of more reactionary viewpoints. The broader social, cultural and political climate can also influence attitudes towards LGBTQ+ people for better or worse.

The general climate towards queer people—both at the macro and micro levels—can impact sexual and gender minorities on a personal level in a profound and material way. A surge in societal bigotry can foster anxiety among queer people and deleteriously impact their mental health even if they're in generally supportive environments. A survey of 873 queer adults conducted between March 8-14, 2024 by Data For Progress finds that 53% of LGBTQ+ adults say "anti-LGBTQ+ policies and

---

[41] "Views on LGBTQ Rights in All 50 States: Findings from PRRI's 2023 American Values Atlas," *Public Religion Research Institute*, last modified March 12, 2024, accessed March 13, 2024, https://www.prri.org/research/views-on-lgbtq-rights-in-all-50-states/

rhetoric" has negatively impacted their mental health (with transgender and younger LGBTQ+ people being disproportionately affected).[42] The same Data For Progress survey also reveals 37% of LGBTQ+ adults say "life quality has gotten worse" in the past year, with 65% of transgender adults reporting that their quality of life has gone down compared to 34% of their queer cis counterparts; additionally, 61% of trans adults have heard transphobic speech from peers, 24% have had their gender-affirming healthcare "interrupted or discontinued," and most trans and non-binary people are concerned they'll face harassment and/or discrimination in healthcare (73%), while using the bathroom (43%), and for wearing clothing that matches their gender identity in public (50%).

Anxiety about the toxicity of the sociopolitical climate can potentially be mitigated by systems of support at the state, local and individual levels, but queer people that lack support structures tend to feel changes in the social climate the most. For example, Oklahoma's Governor, Kevin Stitt, signed a bill into law requiring students to use the bathroom of their sex assigned at birth. Subsequently, Oklahoma Superintendent Ryan Walters appointed Chaya Raichik of Libs of TikTok—a designated anti-LGBTQ extremist by the Southern Poverty Law Center[43]—to the state's Library Media Advisory Committee despite the fact that Raichik

---

[42] Kirby Phares, Rob Todaro, Grace Adcox, and Abby Springs, "Anti-LGBTQ+ Policies and Rhetoric Are Harming LGBTQ+ Lives," *Data For Progress*, last modified March 2024, accessed March 29, 2024, https://www.filesforprogress.org/memos/Anti-LGBTQ-Policies-and-Rhetoric-Are-Harming-LGBTQ-Lives.pdf

[43] "Chaya Raichik," *Southern Poverty Law Center*, accessed April 2, 2024, https://www.splcenter.org/fighting-hate/extremist-files/individual/chaya-raichik

ives in California and has no prior experience. This politically motivated appointment came after Raichik incited harassment against Tyler Wrynn, an Owasso teacher that shared a TikTok telling queer youth he accepts them even if their parents reject them. It became a countywide scandal after Raichik shared his TikTok and insinuated—without evidence—he was a child predator (specifically, accusing him of "grooming" kids). Wrynn resigned following Raichik's post.[44] Less than two years later, an indigenous transgender student of the aforementioned teacher, Nex Benedict, died one day after a physical altercation in a girl's bathroom with three older girls that were bullying him. Weeks later the Oklahoma Medical Examiner's Office ruled Benedict's death a suicide caused by the "combined toxicity" of Diphenhydramine and Fluoxetine.[45] The tragedy illustrates how bigoted adults can often foster a toxic climate that culminates in violence towards queer people. If influential adults in positions of power implicitly and explicitly use bigoted, dehumanizing language towards queer people, young cis and straight people can and often *do* mimic the behavior of adults. And this isn't conjecture. An analysis from The Washington Post found that hate crimes "more than quadrupled" in states with the most discriminatory LGBTQ+ laws and also reported that "calls to

---

[44] Alexia Aston, "As Owasso student dies after school beating, critics blame negativity from 'Libs of TikTok'," *The Oklahoman*, last modified February 21, 2024, accessed February 25, 2024, https://www.oklahoman.com/story/news/2024/02/21/libs-of-tiktok-chaya-raichik-oklahoma-under-fire-after-nonbinary-oklahoma-students-dies/72682329007/

[45] Christopher Wiggins, "Nex Benedict died by suicide, says Oklahoma medical examiner," *Advocate*, last modified March 13, 2024, accessed March 13, 2024, https://www.advocate.com/news/nex-benedict-cause-of-death

LGBTQ+ youth crisis hotlines have exploded."[46] Oklahoma in particular saw a 238% spike in calls by LGBTQ+ youth to the Rainbow Youth Project USA's suicide prevention hotline following the death of Nex Benedict.[47]

The social and political climate towards the LGBTQ+ community in the United States hasn't been this vitriolic for quite some time—arguably since the AIDs crisis—and we're currently witnessing a horrifying race to the bottom across the country. The American Civil Liberties Union tracked more than 500 anti-LGBTQ+ bills in 2023[48] which includes brazenly unconstitutional laws restricting drag performances and pride celebrations. Of the aforementioned 500 anti-LGBTQ+ bills introduced in 2023, over 75 were signed into law (more than doubling the total passed in 2022—the worst legislative year in recorded history for queer people), which prompted the Human Rights Campaign to declare

---

[46] Laura Meckler, Hannah Natanson and John D. Harden, "In states with laws targeting LGBTQ issues, school hate crimes quadrupled," *The Washington Post,* last modified March 12, 2024, accessed March 13, 2024, https://www.washingtonpost.com/education/2024/03/12/school-lgbtq-hate-crimes-incidents/

[47] Mira Lazine, "Calls to LGBTQ+ youth crisis line skyrocket after death of Nex Benedict," *LGBTQ Nation,* last modified March 11, 2024, accessed March 13, 2024, https://www.lgbtqnation.com/2024/03/calls-to-lgbtq-youth-crisis-line-skyrocket-after-death-of-nex-benedict/

[48] "Mapping Attacks on LGBTQ Rights in U.S. State Legislatures in 2023," *ACLU* (American Civil Liberties Union, last modified December 21, 2023, accessed February 25, 2024, https://www.aclu.org/legislative-attacks-on-lgbtq-rights-2023

a "National State of Emergency for LGBTQ+ Americans."[49] 2024 is on track to surpass 2023. By March 1st of 2024, 471 anti-LGBTQ+ bills have been introduced or reintroduced in state legislatures across America.[50] While particular laws in some states were unable to withstand judicial scrutiny—with Texas' drag ban being struck down on grounds that it amounted to an "unconstitutional restriction on speech"[51]—the battle continues across the country, with transgender rights being eroded at an alarming speed. But this trend isn't unique to the United States.

Elected Democrats are comparatively supportive when it comes to LGBTQ+ rights, including trans rights (although a Data for Progress poll found that 79% of LGBTQ+ adults don't think they're doing enough to protect their rights).[52] The same cannot be said about the Labour Party in the United Kingdom, however. The

---

[49] "National State of Emergency for LGBTQ+ Americans," *Human Rights Campaign*, last modified, September 18, 2023, accessed March 29, 2024, https://www.hrc.org/campaigns/national-state-of-emergency-for-lgbtq-americans

[50] "Mapping Attacks on LGBTQ Rights in U.S. State Legislatures in 2024." *ACLU* (American Civil Liberties Union), last modified on March 1, 2024, accessed March 3, 2024, https://www.aclu.org/legislative-attacks-on-lgbtq-rights-2024

[51] Matt Lavietes, "Federal judge declares Texas drag law unconstitutional," *NBC News*, last modified September 26, 2023, accessed February 25, 2024, https://www.nbcnews.com/nbc-out/out-politics-and-policy/federal-judge-declares-texas-drag-law-unconstitutional-rcna117486

[52] Kirby Phares, "LGBTQ+ Adults Do Not Feel Safe and Do Not Think the Democratic Party Is Doing Enough to Protect Their Rights," *Data For Progress*, last modified June 8, 2023, accessed February 25, 2024, https://www.dataforprogress.org/blog/2023/6/8/lgbtq-adults-do-not-feel-safe-and-do-not-think-the-democratic-party-is-doing-enough-to-protect-their-rights

Labour Party is not supportive—and arguably antagonistic—towards trans people, although to a lesser extent than Tories. Typically, social issues such as abortion and gay rights are not as divisive in Great Britain as they are in the United States due to lower levels of religiosity, but when it comes to trans rights, British conservatives are in lockstep with social conservatives in the United States. The media, politicians, and celebrities in Great Britain have otherised and marginalized trans people to the point where it was deemed "one of the worst places to be trans" in Europe following a report by Transgender Europe.[53] Chantele Billson of Pink News explains:

> *Prime minister Rishi Sunak said: "A man is a man, and a woman is a woman, that's just common sense", while health secretary Steve Barclay proposed banning transgender women from female hospital wards, despite a study last year revealing that there had not been a single complaint about the issue.*[54]

Worse, Prime Minister Rishi Sunak has been particularly callous towards trans people in the face of an increasingly violent climate in the country. Brianna Ghey, an openly transgender teenager, was brutally murdered in a hate crime[55] that garnered international

---

[53] Chantelle Billson, "UK one of the worst places to be trans, with 'widespread' hatred, new data shows," *Pink News*, last modified November 1, 2023, accessed February 25, 2024, https://www.thepinknews.com/2023/11/01/uk-worst-place-to-be-trans/

[54] See citation in previous footnote.

[55] Helen Pidd, "Teenagers jailed for 'exceptionally brutal' murder of Brianna Ghey," *The Guardian*, last modified February 2, 2024, accessed February 25, 2024, https://www.theguardian.com/uk-news/2024/feb/02/brianna-ghey-murderers-named-sentenced-to-life-in-prison

attention, but the presence of her family in parliament didn't stop Sunak from making disparaging comments about trans people while they were in attendance. Sunak implied Labour leader Sir Kier Starmer—no ally to trans people—didn't know "how to define a woman," and subsequently denied his comment was bigoted and refused to apologize to Ghey's family for his lack of sensitivity.[56]

But while this level of cruelty is unsurprising from the U.K.'s Conservatives, one might expect Labour to be better—and they *are* marginally better in *some* ways—but that in no way means they're supportive of trans rights. Sir Kier Starmer has opposed basic civil rights for trans people in defiance of Labour's voter base (a majority of which supports trans people and basic rights for them[57]) and his adversarial stance towards trans people has been so divisive it lead to a split between the Scottish Labour Party and the national Labour Party[58] after he whipped votes[59]

---

[56] Archie Mitchell, "Sunak again refuses to apologise to Brianna Ghey's family for transgender jibe," *Independent*, last modified February 9, 2024, accessed February 25, 2024, https://www.independent.co.uk/news/uk/politics/rishi-sunak-trans-joke-brianna-ghey-b2493493.html

[57] Ell Folan, "The numbers don't lie – Labour is woefully out of touch with its own voters on trans rights," *Pink News*, last modified August 21, 2023, accessed March 4, 2024, https://www.thepinknews.com/2023/08/21/labour-party-keir-starmer-trans-rights/

[58] "Sir Keir Starmer and Scottish Labour split over self-ID for trans people," *BBC*, last modified July 26, 2023, accessed February 25, 2024, https://www.bbc.com/news/uk-scotland-scotland-politics-66315485

[59] Ell Folan, "The numbers don't lie – Labour is woefully out of touch with its own voters on trans rights," *Pink News*, last modified August 21, 2023, accessed March 4, 2024, https://www.thepinknews.com/2023/08/21/labour-party-keir-starmer-trans-rights/

against the Scottish National Party's gender reform bill that would've granted basic recognition to trans Brits. In 2024 things got even worse. England's National Health System (NHS) announced it would no longer prescribe puberty blockers to minors diagnosed with gender dysphoria, claiming there was a dearth of evidence when it comes to "the safety or clinical effectiveness" of the treatment[60] despite strong evidence to the contrary which finds that gender-affirming care for minors can be life-saving. A meta-analysis by The Trevor Project confirms puberty blockers are particularly effective at improving body image and emotional issues while simultaneously decreasing long-term suicidality.[61] While the U.K. is particularly bad when it comes to trans rights, anti-trans hysteria has spread throughout Europe and even Scandinavia.

A Global Trend of Regression

The Western world isn't alone in its regression on LGBTQ+ rights. Authoritarian countries like Uganda and Russia have both enacted harsher restrictions on LGBTQ+ people in the '20s than they did in the '10s. Russia not only recently expanded their prohibition of LGBTQ+ "propaganda," they also designated the LGBTQ+ movement as "extremist" and added it to their state

---

[60] Tara John, "England's health service to stop prescribing puberty blockers to transgender kids," CNN, last modified March 13, 2024, accessed March 13, 2024, https://www.cnn.com/2024/03/13/uk/england-nhs-puberty-blockers-trans-children-intl-gbr/index.html

[61] "Gender-Affirming Care for Youth," *The Trevor Project*, last modified January 29, 2020, accessed March 13, 2024, https://www.thetrevorproject.org/research-briefs/gender-affirming-care-for-youth/

ist of terrorists alongside groups like Al Qaeda.[62] Ghana's parliament passed legislation making it illegal to identify as LGBTQ+ or advocate for them.[63] Queer people in autocratic countries don't have the privilege of pressuring or protesting their governments; and doing so could literally be deadly, which often forces them to flee their countries in order to be free. But fleeing one's country doesn't necessarily mean they'll live happily ever after, unfortunately. Eden Knight, a 23-year-old Saudi Arabian transgender woman studying in the United States, tragically committed suicide after she was coerced into returning home to Saudi Arabia, where her parents forced her to detransition.[64]

While most of the world remains deeply bigoted against the LGBTQ+ community, not every country is trending in a negative direction. Greece finally legalized same-sex marriages in 2024. Thailand's House of Representatives voted overwhelmingly

[62] "Russia adds 'LGBT movement' to list of extremist and terrorist organisations," *Reuters*, last modified March 22, 2024, accessed March 26, 2024, https://www.reuters.com/world/europe/russia-adds-lgbt-movement-list-extremist-terrorist-organisations-2024-03-22/

[63] Gabriella Ferlita, "Ghana passes sweeping bill making identifying as LGBTQ+ or campaigning for queer rights illegal," *Pink News*, last modified Feb. 29, 2024, accessed March 3, 2024, https://www.thepinknews.com/2024/02/29/ghana-passes-anti-lgbt-bill/?utm_content
=1709166832&utm_medium=social&utm_source=twitter

[64] Miles Klee, "Saudi Trans Woman's Devastating Suicide Note Leaves Her Community Outraged," *Rolling Stone*, last modified March 16, 2023, accessed February 25, 2024, https://www.rollingstone.com/culture/culture-features/eden-knight-saudi-trans-suicide-1234698274/

(400-10) in favor of legalizing marriage equality.[65] Additionally, there's been a significant shift in public support for marriage equality in Japan with 63% of the population supporting the legalization of same-sex marriages.[66] Moreover, Japan's Sapporo High Court recently declared same-sex marriage restrictions unconstitutional, with Judge Kiyofumi Saito calling such bans "discrimination that lacks rationality."[67] While The Sapporo High Court of Japan's ruling did not legalize same-sex marriages (for the fact that it does not have the power of judicial review like the U.S. Supreme Court), the ruling could help LGBTQ+ activists overcome the inertia of Japan's bicameral legislature (known collectively as the National Diet). This is one of many judicial victories for same-sex couples in Japan, but the Sapporo High Court's ruling goes further than lower-level courts that ruled

---

[65] Kocha Olarn and Helen Regan, "Thailand's lower house passes bill to legalize same-sex marriage," *CNN*, last modified March 27, 2024, accessed March 27, 2024, https://www.cnn.com/2024/03/27/asia/thailand-passes-marriage-equality-bill-intl-hnk/index.html

[66] Craig Kafura, "Japan's Public Is Ready for Change on LGBTQ Rights. Is the Government?," *The Chicago Council on Global Affairs*, last modified June 15, 2023, accessed February 25, 2024, https://globalaffairs.org/commentary-and-analysis/blogs/japans-public-ready-change-lgbtq-rights-government#:~:text=Japanese%20Public%20Broadly%20Supportive%20of%20Marriage%20Equalit y&text=Most%20recently%2C%20an%20April%202023,especially%20strong %20among%20younger%20Japanese

[67] Mari Yamaguchi, "A Japanese court says denying same-sex marriage is unconstitutional and calls for urgent change," Associated Press, last modified March 14, 2024, accessed March 16, 2024, https://apnews.com/article/japan-lgbtq-samesex-marriage-ruling-court-f869fa7d2b22bfc1eafcd5d6a7c9d5a2#:~:te xt=TOKYO%20(AP)%20—%20A%20Japanese,hope%20for%20change%20to ward%20equality

against same-sex marriage bans while not plainly deeming them unconstitutional.[68]

However unresponsive democratic countries may be when it comes to queer rights, the mere *notion* of even decriminalizing homosexuality and trans/non-binary identities is a nonstarter for many socially conservative authoritarian governments around the world. As a result, sexual and gender minorities in these countries are forced to adapt to the hostile political climate by pressuring their governments covertly; but this new wave of queer activism has only been made possible within the last couple of decades thanks to an increase in internet access and widespread use of cell phones. For example, queer activists in the Middle East and North Africa have been able to form and sustain sizable LGBTQ+ rights movements by using the internet almost exclusively. In fact, the internet has arguably been a stronger catalyst for new social movements than liberalization *and even democratization itself.*

The Utility of the Internet for New Social Movements

Online activism—sometimes referred to derisively as "slacktivism"—has negative connotations in the West, but in regions of the world where civil liberties and civil rights are essentially non-existent, progressive social movement organizations (SMOs) *cannot* exist without the internet. The internet has fundamentally transformed political activism and expanded possibilities in most regions of the world. This book tracks the rise of these movements in Morocco, Algeria, and Tunisia in a case study that demonstrates how the internet has not

---

[68] See citation in previous footnote.

only *transformed* the nature of social movements, but made them *possible* in regimes where such activism is strictly prohibited.

Unfortunately, since the research in this book was originally published, many governments—both authoritarian *and* democratic—have become cognizant of the internet's role in political activism and have doubled down on restrictions in an effort to maintain control over increasingly dissatisfied populations. While this book focuses primarily on non-democracies in the MENA region, new censorious internet restrictions by democratic governments have become commonplace as well. To make matters worse, employers are also increasingly exerting control over the political speech of their employees, especially with respect to their social media activity.

On the issue of Israel and Palestine alone, online advocacy has been met with rampant censorship and abuse; Republican lawmakers have called for an outright ban on TikTok in response to widespread "anti-Israel" sentiment on the platform,[69] American journalists who've expressed support for Palestinians in Gaza have been fired,[70] while an Israeli teacher[71] as well as a

---

[69] Makena Kelly, "Republicans demand a ban on lawmakers using TikTok," *The Verge*, last modified April 18, 2023, accessed February 25, 2024, https://www.theverge.com/2023/4/18/23688361/tiktok-ban-congress-republicans-aoc-china-bytedance

[70] Aleks Phillips, "Full List of Journalists Fired Over Pro-Palestinian Remarks," *Newsweek*, last modified October 25, 2023, accessed February 25, 2024, https://www.newsweek.com/full-list-reporters-fired-pro-palestinian-remarks-1837834

[71] Nir Hasson, X (formerly Twitter), @nirhasson, posted November 10, 2023, accessed February 25, 2024, https://twitter.com/nirhasson/status/1722889913866088713

Palestinian couple in Israel[72] were arrested for social media posts where they expressed sympathy for innocent Palestinians victimized by Israel's indiscriminate bombing campaign in Gaza in 2023 and 2024.

More insidious forms of online censorship have been pushed as well. The *Kids Online Safety Act* (KOSA) is bipartisan internet legislation in the United States intended to "[apply] pressure on platforms to install filters that would wipe the net of anything deemed 'inappropriate' for minors,"[73] but civil rights groups argue it would very likely harm vulnerable young people in marginalized communities. Opponents of KOSA worry Republican-controlled states could, for instance, use it to censor content tailored for LGBTQ+ youth by designating it as "inappropriate"—or even "pornographic"—which could harm young queer people in need of vital resources. In this vehemently homophobic and transphobic climate that's a valid concern. Even *The Trevor Project*, an organization dedicated to preventing suicides of queer youth, has been attacked and defamed with innuendo suggesting it's a "pedophilia" group.[74] Self-proclaimed "theocratic fascist" commentator Matt Walsh of The Daily Wire falsely claimed The Trevor Project hosted "sexually explicit chat

---

[72] Al Jazeera English, X (formerly Twitter), @AJEnglish, posted November 9, 2023, accessed February 25, 2024, https://twitter.com/AJEnglish/status/1722631983816470760

[73] Fight For The Future, "Why is KOSA a bad bill?," stopkosa.com, accessed, February 25, 2024, https://www.stopkosa.com/

[74] Al Ferguson, "Right-Wing Declares War On 'The Trevor Project', Labels it 'Pedophilia'," *Queer News Tonight*, streamed May 5, 2022, accessed February 25, 2024, https://www.youtube.com/watch?v=x7DcMLUK_lM

room[s] that connects children as young as 13 years old with 'LGBT' adults."[75] In reality experienced LGBTQ+ adult counselors are connected to queer youth who are at risk of self-harm and suicide[76] to council and dissuade them harming themselves, not to "groom" or sexually prey on them. Nevertheless, hate directed at The Trevor Project drove them off of platforms[77] like X (formerly Twitter) entirely. It wouldn't be unreasonable to assume KOSA could be used to restrict queer youth's access to life-saving resources like The Trevor Project for the fact that one of the bill's sponsors, Republican Senator Marsha Blackburn, implied KOSA could be used to protect "minor children from the transgender" influence in American culture.[78]

In addition to KOSA, the Foreign Adversary Controlled Applications Act (FACAA), which would effectively ban TikTok in the United States, passed overwhelmingly in the U.S. House of Representatives with both Republican and Democratic support

---

[75] This is a quote from a viral post on X (formerly Twitter) by popular conservative commentator and self-proclaimed "theocratic fascist" Matt Walsh (@mattwalshblog,) on June 15, 2023. See: https://twitter.com/MattWalshBlog/status/1669457292968828928?lang=en (Accessed February 25, 2024).

[76] "Facts About Suicide Among LGDTQ+ Young People," *The Trevor Project*, last modified December 15, 2021, accessed February 25, 2024, https://www.thetrevorproject.org/resources/article/facts-about-lgbtq-youth-suicide/

[77] Brooke Sopelsa and Jo Yurcaba, "LGBTQ youth suicide prevention group leaves X after uptick in 'hate & vitriol'," *NBC News*, last modified November 9, 2023, accessed February 25, 2024, https://www.nbcnews.com/nbc-out/out-news/lgbtq-youth-suicide-prevention-group-leaves-x-uptick-hate-vitriol-rcna124501

[78] "Sen. Marsha Blackburn's Top Priority is Social Media. Here's Why." *Family Policy Alliance*, posted September 1, 2023, accessed March 3, 2024, https://www.youtube.com/watch?v=jg21OdmUj1g.

ust eight days after it was introduced by Republican lawmaker Mike Gallagher. FACAA would prohibit Apple and Google's app stores from offering TikTok if the company fails to divest from its Chinese parent company, ByteDance, within six months. While the text of the legislation was clearly written to target TikTok, FACAA would give the President broad authority to potentially ban other websites as well, thus opening the door to more censorship down the road. Most lawmakers support FACAA under the pretense that TikTok could pose a potential threat to U.S. national security; however, this legislation was sponsored after months of allegations from pro-Israel lawmakers that the app was purposefully promoting pro-Palestinian content in a coordinated campaign to drive down support for Israel. There is no evidence to substantiate this claim, and the popularity of pro-Palestinian viewpoints is entirely organic. As Rebecca Jennings argued in an article for Vox prior to FACAA's passage:

> *Instead of considering the popularity of pro-Palestine content to be a bellwether for young people's attitudes, people in power continue to blame the platforms themselves, using the fact that TikTok's parent company is based in China as evidence it's pushing leftist propaganda.*[79]

This fundamental misunderstanding of TikTok's algorithm is emblematic of the cognitive dissonance of most U.S. lawmakers. They are out of step with the public, and rather than changing their policies to align with voters, they are instead opting to scapegoat just one social media app in a thinly veiled attempt to

---

[79] Rebecca Jennings, "TikTok isn't creating false support for Palestine. It's just reflecting what's already there.," *Vox*, last modified December 13, 2023, accessed March 16, 2024, https://www.vox.com/culture/23997305/tiktok-palestine-israel-gaza-war

quash dissent. The U.S. is not the first government to opt for censorship during a legitimacy crisis and they won't be the last.

To the extent that young people are being "radicalized" by TikTok, it is not the result of a conspiracy or coordinated campaign by the Chinese government; rather, it is the result of a generational divide driven by differences in news consumption. Younger people are more likely[80] to get their news from social media websites and see firsthand accounts of suffering in Gaza, whereas older generations still predominantly consume news through more traditional, corporate-filtered methods that "heavily"[81] favor Israel and fail to humanize Palestinians. Younger people, generally, are more socially conscious and view U.S. support for Israel's 2023-2024 siege on Gaza—argued to be tantamount to genocide by the South African government in the International Court of Justice—as morally indefensible. U.S. lawmakers, however, perceive this disconnect as a propaganda problem as opposed to a policy problem, hence why they've opted to change perceptions via censorship in lieu of changing policy, as Jennings pointed out. But FACAA is just one of numerous anti-TikTok bills cooked up by U.S. lawmakers for dubious reasons.

As politicians in the United States, Canada, the United Kingdom and elsewhere regularly propose new laws restricting internet freedom in various ways, non-democracies have

---

[80] "Social Media and News Fact Sheet," *Pew Research Center*, last modified November 15, 2023, accessed March 16, 2024, https://www.pewresearch.org/journalism/fact-sheet/social-media-and-news-fact-sheet/

[81] Adam Johnson and Othman Ali, "Coverage of Gaza War in the New York Times and Other Major Newspapers Heavily Favored Israel, Analysis Shows," *The Intercept*, last modified January 9, 2024, accessed March 16, 2024, https://theintercept.com/2024/01/09/newspapers-israel-palestine-bias-new-york-times/

expectedly ramped up internet censorship too. For example, China has been battling with citizens trying to skirt internet regulations for years.[82] Iran has imposed "digital curfews"[83] on users in response to widespread protests following the death of Mahsa Amini, a Kurdish woman who died while she was in custody of Iranian police after being arrested for wearing her hijab improperly. But these two anecdotal examples barely scratch the surface.

The use of virtual private networks (VPNs) has exploded, with approximately 1.6 billion people[84] now using them. VPNs are used for a plethora of reasons (e.g. to protect data, access the internet in different regions, etc.), but it's fair to assume their surge in popularity is—at least in part—attributable to new internet restrictions imposed by governments around the globe. The changing nature of internet freedom is a testament to the increasingly important role the web plays in politics around the world. Its capacity to facilitate the free flow of information, collective action and advocacy is increasingly perceived as a threat to all kinds of governments. Citizens dissatisfied with

---

[82] Joy Dog, "China's Internet Censors Try a New Trick: Revealing Users' Locations," *The New York Times*, last modified May 18, 2022, accessed February 25, 2024, https://www.nytimes.com/2022/05/18/business/china-internet-censors-ip-address.html

[83] Sanam Mahoozi, "FEATURE-Iran steps up internet crackdown one year after Mahsa Amini death," *Reuters*, last modified September 13, 2023, accessed March 3, 2024, https://www.reuters.com/article/iran-protests/feature-iran-steps-up-internet-crackdown-one-year-after-mahsa-amini-death-idINL8N3AJ203

[84] Niki Mizuguchi, "VPN growth highlights global crackdown on internet freedom," *Nikkei Asia*, last modified October 1, 2023, accessed February 25, 2024, https://asia.nikkei.com/Business/Technology/VPN-growth-highlights-global-crackdown-on-internet-freedom

unresponsive democratic governments can use the internet to streamline political activism, whereas citizens in non-democracies can utilize it to challenge power in an incognito manner with little to no cost.

LGBTQ+ Movements in the MENA and the Internet

As the tenth anniversary of the this book approaches, I'm delighted to know students around the globe still download it on a monthly basis. I've decided to re-release it for a broader audience in hopes that it will inspire others to continue my work, or perhaps start new research of their own. Prior to the publication of the 2nd edition of this book, it has only been available to students with access to academic search engines such as ProQuest, but now it's available digitally and in print for the first time! This research project started as a graduate research paper before it turned into my Master's thesis and was ultimately published as a book. Like all academic articles and books, this one can feel redundant, technical and dense at times, but I'm confident it's still accessible to most people.

Considering the global decline of democracy and rise of homophobia—and especially transphobia in the United States, the United Kingdom, Canada and elsewhere—I feel like this work is more important today than it was nearly ten years ago. The purpose of this book is to showcase the crucial role the internet plays in modern-day social movements. It was written in 2015 in the aftermath of the Arab spring in 2011. Though the extent to which social media (namely, Facebook) played a role in the Arab spring is still debated, there's no doubt it at least played *some* role.[85] And with regard to LGBTQ+ advocacy in the region, the internet's role has been *integral*. Myths about queerness being an exclusively Western phenomenon have been debunked by queer people in these countries coming out to the world. Moreover, misconceptions about there being no appetite whatsoever for social justice and postmaterialist causes in the Middle East and North Africa have been shattered by this research. While security and access to food and water remain more salient than gender equality or queer rights to people in the MENA, there *is* a growing appetite for social issues, particularly from marginalized communities. Obviously, queer people exist in literally every country on Earth, and like all of us, they want—and deserve—full legal and social equality too.

An Interesting Puzzle in North Africa

In this book, I solve a puzzle I encountered while studying LGBTQ+ rights in the MENA region: why was queer activism so much more prominent in Morocco and Algeria than in Tunisia until the 2010s? On its face it doesn't make sense. Tunisia is a much more socially liberal country, whereas Morocco and Algeria in contrast are far more socially conservative. One would assume queer activists in Tunisia's comparatively liberal society would have capitalized on that climate and staked their claim earlier, but queer rights activists in Morocco and Algeria had a head start, and thus, developed more robust movements than their Tunisian neighbors by the 2010s. That changed when Tunisia democratized,

---

[85] Heather Brown, Emily Guskin and Amy Mitchell, "The Role of Social Media in the Arab Uprisings," *Pew Research Center*, last modified November 28, 2012, accessed February 25, 2024, https://www.pewresearch.org/journalism/2012/11/28/role-social-media-arab-uprisings/

but liberalization was only indirectly responsible for the materialization of Tunisia's LGBTQ+ movement. The *actual* catalyst for these movements, as I discovered in 2015, was the internet; its availability, levels of internet freedom, and access to smart phones.

It's possible other factors explain postmaterial social movement organizations (SMOs) in the MENA region better than internet access, and I lay out alternate explanations and additional variables in the final chapter. But, in the specific region I examined, it is clear that the internet played a pivotal role in the formation of queer social justice movements. This finding matters because if the survival of SMOs in certain regions hinges on a free and open internet, then it logically follows that we must safeguard, preserve and treat the internet as the precious *political resource* that it is specifically as a means of protecting burgeoning social movements born online. The digital rights movement, therefore, is *an important social movement in and of itself,* since the internet has become a crucial conduit for activism in the 21st century. As global capitalism continues to facilitate the destruction of our planet, western democracies continue to decline, and authoritarian regimes in the global south consolidate power and restrict civil liberties even further, I predict the internet will become an even *more* important tool for political activism in the coming decades.

Those who've followed *The Humanist Report* for a while know that issues pertaining to internet freedom (such as net neutrality) and LGBTQ+ rights have been incredibly close to my heart. My findings from this book, in part, explain why I care so much about these two issues. We use the internet to find employment, work, do homework, make connections, listen to music, consume content, shop and have mind-numbingly stupid debates. I mean, I have *my own show* because the internet democratized news. The internet has become an inextricable part of modern human existence, so it's no surprise it is invaluable within the realm of politics too. I set out to make that case in this book, and I genuinely hope you find it insightful. *Enjoy!*

CHAPTER 1

The Emergence of LGBTQ+ Movements in the MENA

Governments in the Middle East and North Africa (MENA) have dismal reputations internationally for authoritarianism and lack of political reform. Overt corruption, restrictions on civil liberties, and gross violations of human rights are commonplace in the region. These aspects of authoritarian governance are merely a snapshot of an exhaustive catalog of problems that hinder regional peace and stability, as societal issues such as sectarian violence, political cleavages, and widespread religious fundamentalism also contributes to much of the turmoil that plagues these states. Moreover, colonization, foreign meddling, resource exploitation and western militarism has played a key role in the destabilization of the region as well. Despite the dismal political context for citizens in MENA countries, they are resilient and appear remarkably happy. The World Values Survey (2010-2014, V10) illustrates that an average of 23.9% of respondents in the region claim to be "very happy" and an average of 52.9%—a majority—assert they are "rather happy" (compared to 36.1% and 53.5% in the United States, respectively).[86] The level of happiness of a populace is a good indication that citizens do not feel their political situation is hopeless. Citizens in the MENA region are becoming increasingly politically active even under heavily repressive regimes that attempt to violently stifle demonstrations.

In 2011 citizens in the MENA, from the Sahrawi people in the Western Sahara to the citizens of Saudi Arabia, mobilized in protests. Though some regimes—primarily monarchical ones— proved to be quite resilient, the Arab spring lead to the overthrow of several autocratic dictators: Zine El Abidine Ben Ali in Tunisia, Muammar Gaddafi in Libya[87], and Hosni Mubarak in Egypt. What once seemed unfathomable had finally occurred. These events raise questions about what catalyzed unprecedented social mobilization. Many political scientists contend that technological growth, specifically higher levels of internet penetration, the proliferation of smartphones, and increased access to satellite television channels such as Al Jazeera has fostered conditions that allowed the Arab spring to occur (Lust 2013; Lynch 2012; Hussain & Howard 2013). Lust argues that the internet was a key tool for political mobilization (2013, 283). The internet could also

---

[86] States and territories included in this study are Algeria, Bahrain, Cyprus, Palestine, Iraq, Jordan, Kuwait, Lebanon, Libya, Morocco, Qatar, Tunisia, Egypt, Yemen, and for comparative reasons, the United States (see World Values Survey 2010-2014, V10).

[87] What started as a grassroots uprising in Libya ended in regime change facilitated by the U.S. government. It was referred to as President Obama's "Worst Mistake" in a column written by Dominic Tierney in *The Atlantic* in 2016.

trigger a plethora of political consequences, including the emergence of movements for socially and culturally taboo causes that would not otherwise exist without it.

One of the potential upshots of greater access to the internet is the materialization of lesbian, gay, bisexual, transgender/non-binary, queer/questioning, intersex, asexual/aromantic, pansexual, two-spirit[88], etc. (LGBTQIAP2S)[89] equality movements throughout the region within the last several decades. The strength and overall existence of these movements, however, is not consistent in every state. For example, Morocco and Algeria, two socially conservative and politically repressive states, both have sizable queer rights movements, but the Moroccan LGBTQ+ movement differs in that it is discernibly larger than Algeria's and has existed longer. In Tunisia, a more socially liberal state, LGBTQ+ activism was nonexistent until it underwent democratization. Why did members of the LGBTQ+ community become politically active in two socially conservative authoritarian states (Morocco and Algeria), but not in Tunisia, a more open-minded, secular, and socially liberal authoritarian state?

Theoretically, one should have expected to find a more robust LGBTQ+ movement in Tunisia *before* Morocco and

---

[88] See Glossary.

[89] The extended LGBTQIAP2S acronym is sometimes used to include a broader range of sexual and gender minorities associated with the LGBTQ+ community; however, usage of the '+' in the LGBTQ+ acronym denotes inclusivity of additional queer minorities not explicitly named. Not all of these identities are mutually exclusive (e.g. a transgender woman could also be a lesbian, an asexual person could be non-binary, etc.). In this book we will primarily use LGBTQ+, queer, and/or sex and gender minorities interchangeably to refer to the collective community.

Algeria seeing as how social conservatism is less prevalent there. Issues related to gender equality, alcohol consumption, and secularity are much less controversial in Tunisia in comparison with Morocco and Algeria, but in spite of this fact Tunisia is the last of these three states to witness the emergence of a queer rights movement. What factor explains variation in the size, strength, time of arrival, and, most importantly, the overall existence of LGBTQ+ movements between these three relatively similar states? Solving this puzzle will yield an answer to an even broader question: what catalyzes LGBTQ+ movements in politically repressive authoritarian regimes in the Middle East and North Africa?

My argument is that the advent of new political opportunities (in this case, expanded internet access and internet freedom) explains why queer rights movements are able to emerge in authoritarian regimes. This argument hinges on my findings from Morocco, Algeria, and Tunisia. Variation in the strength and existence of LGBTQ+ movements in these three cases can be attributed to varying degrees of access to the internet and internet freedom in each state. The internet is a crucial resource for queer rights activists in the MENA, therefore limitations on internet access and internet freedom will inhibit their ability to engage in activism. This claim substantiates the resource mobilization school of thought.

This implies that restraints of dictatorial and oppressive governments may no longer be able to hold back political change. Due to citizens' increased access to the internet, advocates for LGBTQ+ rights and other "postmaterialist" causes are able to forge movements that could potentially gain ascendency in the coming decades now that they have the ability to discretely mobilize and collude with like-minded citizens to anonymously petition their governments for a redress of grievances. However, even with the presence of new political opportunities, this type of activism in the MENA region runs contrary to our current theoretical understandings of social movements and why they emerge in the first place.

The Rise of Postmaterialism in the Middle East & North Africa

Many MENA citizens are socioeconomically disadvantaged, therefore one could logically deduce that they will be more inclined to adopt political orientations tailored to their physical (material) well-being as opposed to their social status (postmaterial). To engage in activism for the latter cause would imply its participants hold postmaterialist values. Postmaterialism is defined as a "value orientation that emphasizes self-expression and quality of life over economic and physical security" (Encyclopedia Britannica 2008). The concept of postmaterialism was developed by Inglehart (1977) who postulates that individuals have a hierarchy of values. He states,

> [t]he values of Western publics have been shifting from an overwhelming emphasis on material well-being and physical security toward greater emphasis on the quality of life. [...] People tend to be more concerned with immediate needs or threats than with things that seem remote or nonthreatening. Thus a desire for beauty may be more or less universal, but hungry people are more likely to seek food than aesthetic satisfaction (Ibid. 1990, 5).

43

This indicates states who have not advanced industrially and/or those in which the physical vulnerability of their citizens is high[90] will be unlikely to foster political environments that are conducive to more "modern" or egalitarian views on matters such as civil rights and social equity.

In theory, values that facilitate the emergence of such causes should not be prevalent—or exist at all—in the MENA region according to existing sociological and political science concepts such as modernization theory, but that is not the case. The mere existence of LGBTQ+ activism suggests that egalitarian, socially progressive, and modern views are held by some. The World Values Survey (2010-2014, Y002) measures postmaterialism in the MENA region using 4-item inter-related questions in order to gauge values.[91] It found that a majority of citizens in many MENA states hold mixed material/postmaterialist values, and an average of 5.3% of citizens mostly embrace postmaterialist values (see Table 1.1). This is not surprising when accounting for the recent surge of LGBTQ+ activism in the region.

---

[90] This is perhaps due to territorial disputes, wars, apartheid facilitated by Israel in the West Bank as well as prison-like conditions in Gaza, or high levels of state-sponsored violence or repression in authoritarian regimes.

[91] It should be noted that the methodology for this particular question is not available for this variable, but the World Values Survey is a reputable organization that is cited with regularity in academia. Still, for purposes of this discussion, it would prove beneficial to know how postmaterialism is measured, but the point of bringing this up is merely for illustrative purposes to show that these values do exist in the MENA, albeit to a small degree.

Table 1.1: Postmaterialist Values in the MENA Region

Algeria	Bahrain	Cyprus	Palestine	Iraq	Jordan	Lebanon
5.1%	20.2%	5.8%	5.6%	3.5%	2.6%	7.7%
(44.8%)	(60.5%)	(51%)	(45.8%)	(52.4%)	(37.8%)	(55.2%)
Libya	Morocco	**Qatar**	**Tunisia**	Türkiye	**Egypt**	**Yemen**
4.2%	2.9%	4.7%	.9%	10.7%	1.1%	.9%
(63%)	(42.4%)	(53%)	(25.6%)	(53.3%)	(36.6%)	(28.9%)

Note: Percentages in parentheses indicate mixed postmaterialist and materialist values.
Source: World Values Survey (2010-2014, Y002).

Postmaterialist causes are, in effect, those wherein the primary political objective is to eliminate conditions that diminish the overall quality of living for particular citizens (Ibid.). These causes will typically be related to social equality and may include gay and transgender rights, atheist, agnostic, areligious, anti-theist, and deist (AAAAD)[92] rights, religious rights, indigenous people's rights, and racial/ethnic minorities' rights movements. These examples do not encompass the totality of possible movements for postmaterialist causes, but instead are part of a broader range of postmaterialist issues. Many individuals assume these types of movements, especially those advocating for LGBTQ+ rights, do not exist in conservative, autocratic regimes seeing that they are widely regarded as "taboo" or "haram" and are too controversial to attain political clout, but the recent materialization of LGBTQ+ rights movements in the MENA forces introspection within the social science community since

---

[92] While the terms 'atheist' and 'areligious' may sound redundant, they are differentiated by the fact that atheism is the belief that a god does not exist whereas an areligious individual may believe a god exists, but does not subscribe to a particular religion.

these movements *do* exist; however, the character of these movements differs from their Western counterparts.

Characteristics of Queer Rights Movements in the MENA

The first, and perhaps most significant, difference between Western LGBTQ+ rights movements and those which exist in the global South is short-term goals. In the West, LGBTQ+ activists' short term goals may be full marriage equality and federal anti-discrimination legislation to protect their community from employment discrimination and/or societal prejudice. Their long-term goals will be broader and encapsulate full legal recognition and societal equality. Conversely, the goals of queer rights activists in the MENA region may ultimately coincide with Western LGBTQ+ activists, but they fundamentally differ in one important respect: Western activists possess goals that cannot be feasibly achieved by activists in the MENA. A common short-term goal for LGBTQ+ activists in many MENA countries, for example, is the amelioration of governmental persecution, whereas a common long-term goal is decriminalization of homosexuality and/or the full legal right to practice homosexuality or express one's gender identity freely.

These groups typically establish goals by coalescing around legal and social matters that are most culpable in the perpetuation of their collective marginalization. Given that the mere act of homosexuality is legally prohibited in most MENA states,[93] decriminalization is a common goal for most queer rights activists in the region. This criteria for goal attainment is comparable for Western activists, but they are not reluctant to

---

[93] See Chapter 2, Table 2.1.

demand sweeping reforms. This is a luxury that is afforded to them for living in a democracy with protections for civil liberties. These differences are also dependent on the fact that Western activists have prodigious movements that have persisted for decades, and as a result, they have been able to gain considerable ground in many countries and are now in a position to ask for full recognition of their rights. This is not the case for many movements for postmaterialist causes in the MENA, especially when it comes to the issue of queer rights. LGBTQ+ equality movements in the MENA are still in the early stages of development; but regardless, their growth has been appreciable.

While Middle Eastern and North African LGBTQ+ movements have seen an increase in numbers and have become more organized, they have not made much political or social progress. The Western LGBTQ+ community has been successful in part due to its ability to gain support from heterosexual and cisgender[94] allies—a tactic very much in line with African American civil rights activists who fought for desegregation in the '60s by drawing support from white political allies.

Queer rights activists in the MENA region have diminished standards as well as lower ambitions and expectations in comparison to their Western counterparts for the fact that the prospect of legal marriage equality—let alone the prospect of decriminalizing homosexuality—is currently unachievable to them. This forces MENA activists to adjust their expectations to match short and long-term goals that are actually feasible. Putnam (1988) discusses the notion of a "win-set," which is a concept from the field of international relations that describes how the preferences of a state's domestic constituents establish the

---

[94] Refer to "Cisgender" in the Glossary for the definition of this identity.

parameters of an international agreement. He writes, "[t]he larger the win-set, the more easily he [the chief negotiator acting on behalf of the state] can conclude an agreement, but also the weaker his bargaining position vis-à-vis the other negotiator" (450). While this view is prominent in the game theory research methodology—which is mostly utilized for analyzing strategic interactions between international entities—the concept of win-sets can be useful if we apply it to interactions between social activists and governments.

One can expect LGBTQ+ movements in the MENA to have very large win-sets because they will be willing to except any concession from the government in order to improve their social status even if it is unsatisfactory. Their win-set is large because they lack negotiating power and leverage. Groups do not typically shrink their win-sets until they attain political power, which is adjoined to the level of bargaining power they possess. A group with a small win-set will not be appeased by a piece of legislation that, for instance, prohibits discrimination against gays, lesbians, and bisexuals, but not transgender individuals. Their win-set is small because the list of demands they will willingly accept is shorter. In contrast, groups with larger win-sets are easier to appease since they have a large list of policy concessions that will satisfy them since nearly anything will qualify as a win. Contrarily, the government (i.e. their chief opponent) will have a microscopic win-set for the fact that MENA governments will forego negotiations altogether, as highly disliked and disadvantaged groups do not pose a sufficient threat to their legitimacy. Seeing as how Western LGBTQ+ activists have substantial social and political power in the form of lobbying, their respective governments will be more receptive to their demands for the fact that they pose a direct threat to state legitimacy. Victory may be unattainable in the foreseeable future for LGBTQ+ rights activists in the MENA, but this daunting fact has not kept them from trying.

Amid high costs and a low payoff, there has been a surge in acts of civil disobedience among all types of postmaterialist activists in even the most repressive totalitarian and authoritarian regimes. A Saudi Arabian atheist activist, Raif Badawi, posted an online statement advocating free speech for atheists in spite of the fact that the ensuing penalty for doing so would be severe (Hubbard 2015). Additionally, on the International Day Against Homophobia members of the LGBTQ+ community in Tehran uploaded photographs of themselves with rainbow flags and signs reading "no to homophobia" to Joopea, a popular social networking website in Iran (Fisher 2012). In Egypt, in an act of protest, eight men uploaded a video to YouTube of themselves attending and taking part in a wedding ceremony between a same-sex couple in Nile (Kingsley 2014). One thing these instances of activism all have in common is that they occur through a proxy: the internet.

Political scientists and sociologists must contemplate whether these occurrences of online activism are merely isolated, insignificant, and spurious or rather, that they are occurring due to the arrival of a new political opportunity that was not previously available. I do not believe these instances of activism are insignificant. Quite contrarily, I contend that they signify the initiation of new social movements. Identification of the cause(s) of these new movements will be fruitful for future social science research. LGBTQ+ rights movements in the MENA are fascinating for two reasons: (a) they are the most prevalent of all new movements to proliferate in the region, and (b) their persistent growth and longevity[95] makes them easier to measure.

Research Question & Forecasting Arguments

Why do LGBTQ+ movements emerge in authoritarian regimes in the Middle East and North Africa? This book argues that queer rights movements are more likely to emerge in conservative authoritarian regimes when new political opportunities—namely access to the internet for purposes of political organization—become available. In light of the recent emergence of postmaterialist movements in the MENA, this book examines LGBTQ+ movements in three such cases: Morocco, Algeria, and Tunisia. The following chapter details the low social status of the aggregate LGBTQ+ community in the MENA region. Chapter 3 outlines the strength of LGBTQ+ movements in Morocco, Algeria, and Tunisia. Chapter 4 provides a literature review of competing theoretical explanations as well as arguments outlining what causes new social movements to arise. Chapter 5 introduces hypotheses that explain which factor(s) catalyze queer rights activism in authoritarian regimes.

In the sixth chapter I test my hypotheses by utilizing a most similar systems research design (MSSD) methodology with three relatively similar case studies: Morocco, Algeria, and pre/ post-revolutionary Tunisia. Both Morocco and Algeria are authoritarian states that have fairly large LGBTQ+ movements, but a queer rights movement did not materialize in Tunisia until it democratized in spite of the fact that it is much more socially

---

[95] What I mean by longevity is that these movements have not dissipated over time. Instead, they have all grown since materialization and have yet to disband.

liberal in comparison to the two former states mentioned. I argue that variation between the strength and existence of LGBTQ+ movements in these three states is caused by varying degrees of access to the internet. Moroccans and Algerians had more internet freedom in comparison to Tunisians, hence the reason why queer rights activism did not emerge in Tunisia until after democratization, which is when restrictions on the internet were removed. I also argue that Morocco's LGBTQ+ movement is slightly larger than Algeria's despite comparable levels of internet freedom because Moroccans had greater access to the internet than Algerians while both movements began materializing.

Overall, it will be demonstrated that an underlying level of internet freedom is a necessary prerequisite for this type of activism to emerge. The degree to which a vulnerable group is able to bypass internet restrictions to coordinate with other activists is a significant determinant for a movement's success and existence. If a government is too repressive and aims to stymie any and all types of political activism, a movement may not be able to flourish even if it has adequate access to the internet. This will be detailed more thoroughly in Chapter 7, where I will review the overall findings of this research, its applicability to other movements for postmaterialist causes, and implications it has on social movement research.

Rethinking Activism

Before proceeding it will be necessary to elaborate on what is meant by "online activism" in order to sufficiently make the case that it should be categorized into traditional conceptions of activism and social movements. A social movement is a phenomenon whereby citizens with like-minded interests align and engage in contentious politics by confronting "elites, authorities, and opponents" in order to change the legal and social status quo (Tarrow 2011, 6). Mass protests, boycotts, and various types of strikes are typically associated with existing notions of activism, but online activism is becoming equally instrumental to protesters of all stripes. In the MENA region, queer rights activism occurs almost exclusively through the internet, thus making it seemingly amorphous. However, several types of tactics are easily identifiable and have proven to be quite effective to boot. There is a diverse array of methods employed by online activists, ranging from political declarations via social media, signing of online petitions, coordinated "hashtag" campaigns, and even DDoS attacks on government websites. Dismissing this realm of activism is problematic since the internet is the newest frontier for political activism, and as a result, it will allow us to acquire key insight into the emergence of new social movements in the 21st century. For this to be possible, our conceptions of what constitutes social movements must evolve to accommodate it, especially if we are going to measure new types of social movements in authoritarian regimes.

Bayat (2005) calls for "a more fluid and fragmented vision of social movements" by "attempting to present an angle which might help account for complexities" (893). I also hold this view. Though the chief method in which LGBTQ+ activism occurs in the MENA (via online) is admittedly unorthodox, the dawn of the technological era requires us to update our preconceived notions of what constitutes "activism" or a "social movement" because LGBTQ+ activism in most MENA states—for the time being—is inextricably tethered to the internet.[96] Bayat writes, "[g]iven the

---

[96] This will be addressed in the following chapters.

fragmented nature of contemporary social movements, [...] a plausible narrative would take account of the heterogenous layers of perceptions, discourses and practices within a given movement" (905). Following this logic, online activism should be incorporated into our discussion of social movements.

Seeing as how the internet is a launching point for queer rights movements in the MENA, it is beneficial to differentiate between different 'tiers' of activism and hierarchically arrange these movements by size and type before proceeding. Categorization of online activism into different tiers is necessary in order to distinguish between varying levels of strength in movements and also to account for various forms of online political protests that become more coordinated and complex as movements grow. Online activism should be mapped onto a spectrum and cannot be arbitrarily dichotomized. In total there are four tiers that outline and define the parameters of activism that take place under authoritarian regimes on the internet (see Table 1.2). As the size and strength of these movements grow they will advance to subsequent tiers.

States that encompass the lowest level of online activism (titled 'Tier 1') contain minimal amounts of isolated incidents of civil disobedience and instances of activism that are typically sporadic and not necessarily catalyzed by a particular causal mechanism. This may include occasional proclamations on social media of one's sexual, secular, or gender identity. Due to the improbability of such events, they may attract significant amounts of domestic and/or international attention, but not enough to warrant political mobilization among the aggregate group. This includes the establishment of some advocacy-oriented pages on social media, but most of which will be insufficient at drawing in much attention. These instances are likely rare and isolated due to heavy censorship on the internet and the repressive nature of a government.

Tier 2 activism is primarily done through social media, but these acts garner a sufficient amount of domestic attention and include "hashtag" campaigns whereby activists get a specific message to trend or create advocacy-based social media accounts and websites that center around a message of equality. Tier 2 movements are moderately organized. Some coordination is involved in the execution of these campaigns. It is important to factor in the level of attention that online activism gets for the fact that it will contribute to the said group's level of clout and ultimately help them muster much needed public awareness for their cause. Tier 2 movements are able to more freely organize due to either: (a) increased levels of internet freedom, or (b) the ability to bypass governmental restrictions in states with lower levels of internet freedom, as is the case in some MENA states. The LGBTQ+ movement in Iran is able to thrive because activists are able to circumvent governmental firewalls by using a variety of popular software applications (Lee 2013).

When a group's movement has become large, organized and successful enough to be classified as Tier 3, the movement at that point has become more united and has transcended the internet in some ways. At this point the activism has lead to the proliferation of more formal organizations that are headquartered in less repressive countries. Tier 3 movements also witness the creation of multiple informal online organizations and even magazines (that are either available online or distributed furtively). Most importantly, Tier 3 activists have attained support from some prominent domestic and international allies such as celebrities or nongovernmental organizations. It is unlikely that a movement can advance to Tier 3 unless a considerable level of internet freedom is granted to citizens.

Once a movement has advanced to Tier 4 not much of the tactics and mobilization methods have changed from Tier 3, but the group has, at this point, garnered a sufficient amount of political capital and now has the capacity to influence policy either directly themselves or by procuring/co-opting support from powerful political interests such as state oligarchs, politicians, political parties, organizations and/or corporations. Tier 4 movements have the capacity to challenge their state's legitimacy, so the internet is no longer inherently necessary for the movement's existence even if it continues to be their primary tool for organizing. As movements progress to higher tiers their win-sets can be expected to decrease, and conversely, the government's win-set is expected to increase for the fact that the said group in question will pose a larger threat to the social status quo at higher tiers. Tier 4 movements are not common in the MENA, as it requires a regime to be fairly liberalized, if not nominally democratic. This framework is designed to encompass online activism in all authoritarian regimes, so it may also be utilized outside of the MENA region and will be particularly applicable to Sub-Saharan Africa. Categorization of these groups into tiers should not detract from the fact that postmaterialist activism in authoritarian regimes must be measured on a spectrum. While Moroccan and Algerian LGBTQ+ activists, for example, can both be designated as Tier 3, Moroccan activists have progressed further towards the fourth tier than Algerian activists.[97]

---

[97] See Chapter 3, Table 3.1.

Table 1.2: Four Tiers of Online Activism in Authoritarian Regimes

Tier 1	Tier 2	Tier 3	Tier 4
Isolated Instances of Online Civil Disobedience Individual Advocacy-Based Facebook Pages or Twitter Accounts	Coordination of Social Media Campaigns (e.g. "Hashtag" Campaigns) Emergence of Some Informal Online Organizations Mobilization Among the Collective Group Ability to Garner Moderate Amounts of Attention for the Cause	Many Informal Organizations Proliferate Several Formal Advocacy or Outreach-Based Organizations Emerge Outside of the Movement's Home State Group May Have Its Own Broadcast or Publication Group Has Gained Both Domestic and International Allies to Speak on Its Behalf	Tier 3 Tactics Remain Constant, but Group has Now Attained Political Power Group has Co-Opted Politicians and/or Political Parties Group Now Poses a Threat to the State's Legitimacy Group is Able to Pressure Governments to Grant Some Policy Concessions

CHAPTER 2

The Social Status of Sexual & Gender Minorities

Members of the LGBTQ+ community in the Middle East and North Africa are quite possibly more vulnerable and susceptible to prejudice than anywhere else in the world. They are subjected to two forms of discrimination: state-sponsored legal persecution and societal marginalization. Out of twenty-two MENA states and territories[98] homosexuality is only legal in five[99]; male homosexuality is legally prohibited in seventeen of

---

[98] The states and territories examined are Algeria, Bahrain, Cyprus, Egypt, Iran, Iraq, Israel, Jordan, Kuwait, Lebanon, Libya, Mauritania, Morocco, Oman, Palestine, Qatar, Saudi Arabia, Syria, Tunisia, Türkiye, U.A.E. and Yemen.

[99] Homosexuality is legal in Bahrain, Cyprus, Israel, Jordan, Lebanon and Türkiye (see BBC 2014).

them[100], whereas female homosexuality is seemingly illegal in thirteen states,[101] although it should be noted that laws regarding female homosexuality are ambiguous[102] (Itaborahy and Zhu 2014; BBC 2014). While Egypt has not technically criminalized homosexuality, it prosecutes gay people under an anti-debauchery clause, therefore it is reasonable to designate the status of homosexuality as illegal there too (Lee and Sirgany 2015).

The penalty for violating anti-homosexuality laws in the MENA ranges from fines to imprisonment and even death in some states. Homosexuality is punishable by death in thirteen states in the world; however, six of those states (Iran, Qatar, U.A.E., Saudi Arabia, Yemen and Mauritania) are in the MENA, with ambiguous laws in Qatar and the United Arab Emirates likely permitting capital punishment for homosexuality in certain circumstances (BBC 2014, USA Today 2019).[103] No states in the MENA allow same-sex couples to legally marry, although Israel recognizes same-sex marriages performed abroad. In a first for the

---

[100] Male homosexuality is illegal in Algeria, Egypt, Iran, Iraq, Kuwait, Libya, Mauritania, Morocco, Oman, the Palestinian territories, Qatar, Saudi Arabia, Syria, Tunisia, U.A.E. and Yemen (Itaborahy and Zhu 2014).

[101] Female homosexuality is illegal in Algeria, Iran, Kuwait, Libya, Mauritania, Morocco, Oman, Qatar, Saudi Arabia, Syria, U.A.E. and Yemen (Ibid.)

[102] States in which laws regarding female homosexuality are "unclear" includes Egypt and Iraq according to Itaborahy and Zhu (2014). It is also not clear if female homosexuality is still legal in the Palestinian territories and Tunisia, and reports are conflicting for the fact that laws are vague, and women could be prosecuted for homosexuality under laws not explicitly related to the offense.

[103] The other three states where homosexuality is punishable by death is Nigeria, Sudan, Brunei, Afghanistan, Pakistan and Somalia (BBC 2014, USA Today 2019).

Arab world, Tunisia indirectly recognized a same-sex marriage between a French national and Tunisian citizen in 2020 according to Shams, a Tunisian LGBTQ+ group (Weinthal 2020); although Mawjoudin, a different Tunisian LGBTQ+ organization, called it an "administrative mistake" and said it was "wrong and 'disappointing'" for news outlets to sensationalize the story for the fact that it lead to "queerphobic speech, attacks and bullying" (Alturi 2020).

Table 2.1: The Legality of Homosexuality in the Middle East and North Africa

Legal	Legal (Women Only)	Illegal	Punishable By Death
Bahrain	Egypt	Algeria	Iran
Cyprus	Iraq	Iran	Mauritania
Israel	Palestine	Kuwait	Qatar
Jordan	Tunisia	Lebanon	Saudi Arabia
Türkiye		Libya	U.A.E.
		Mauritania	Yemen
		Morocco	
		Oman	
		Qatar	
		Saudi Arabia	
		Syria	
		U.A.E.	
		Yemen	

Source: Itaborahy and Zhu 2014; BBC 2014, USA Today 2019.

With respect to gender identity—although information on legal framework is sparse—five states do not criminalize transgender identities: Cyprus, Israel, Kuwait, Türkiye, and Iran. The Associated Press (2022) reports Kuwait's law prohibiting "imitation of the opposite sex," which criminalized trans existence, was recently struck down by the state's constitutional court. While trans identities may be permissible in the aforementioned states, that does not necessarily mean transgender people have legal recognition. Only four states in the MENA region explicitly allow individuals to undergo gender confirmation surgery (GCS): Cyprus, Israel, Türkiye, and Iran (TGEU 2014a; Oldershausen 2012). There are isolated instances where trans women have been allowed to undergo GCS in countries where the practice is typically banned. Hiba, a trans Syrian woman, was permitted to have GCS after an Iraqi cleric approved the procedure after she passionately plead her case to him, but it is unclear where the procedure was conducted or how often these exceptions are made (GME 2004). In 2022 Cyprus approved legislation granting legal recognition to transgender citizens, although it prohibits gender-affirming care for minors aged sixteen and under unless gender dysphoria becomes "life-threatening" and such care is approved by a Family Court (see Financial Mirror 2022). Prior to these changes, Cyprus already codified anti-discrimination measures for transgender individuals. Besides Israel and Cyprus, it is unknown whether any other states in the region offer protections against discrimination based on gender identity (TGEU 2014a). No state in the region has legally recognized non-binary identities, nor have they codified anti-discrimination protections for non-binary[104] people (TGEU 2014b), although non-binary individuals may marginally benefit from certain laws pertaining to male and female trans people in Kuwait, Cyprus, Israel and possibly Türkiye. Under Egyptian law it is legal to prosecute an individual with an androgynous gender, an alternative gender, or for having no gender identity (Ibid.). The

---

[104] See "Non-Binary Gender Identity" and "Gender Identity" in Glossary for definitions.

extent to which other states have the statutory authority to prosecute people based on deviations from the binary gender system is unknown.

Even upon the repeal of statutes that disproportionately disadvantage members of the LGBTQ+ community, the social climate will not necessarily become less toxic. In Iran, Ayatollah Khomeini—who is vehemently anti-gay—is a proponent of transgender rights (Tait 2005). Zarindast and Hashemi (2012) reports that the regime legally mandates insurance companies to cover the entire cost of gender confirmation surgery,[105] but in spite of governmental support, transgender Iranians still encounter a gratuitous amount of societal discrimination and are frequently perceived to be cross dressers (Dehghan 2012). Furthermore, transgender Iranians are only granted legal recognition after they undergo gender confirmation surgery[106] and could be accused of homosexuality during their transition or before they are fully recognized by the government (Bagri 2017). Though the Iranian government supports and subsidizes hormone replacement therapy (HRT) and gender confirmation surgeries for trans people; it is, nonetheless, *very* hostile towards other members of the LGBTQ+ community, as cisgender queers can be forced to transition in

---

[105] Also referred to as gender affirming surgery (GAS) bottom surgery (BS) or sexual reassignment surgery (SRS). A double mastectomy for trans men is sometimes referred to as top surgery (TS). Not all trans people opt for surgeries. Many trans people who prefer surgery are unable to get it in countries like the United States where it is cost prohibitive, thus forcing many trans people to create GoFundMe accounts to raise money from friends and family to fund them. GoFundMe, however, is not unique to trans Americans, as many people are forced to create GoFundMe accounts in the aftermath of medical emergencies.

[106] For more details about Iran's legal framework surrounding transgender rights, see "Outright International" in the references.

order to evade the death penalty if they are charged with homosexuality (Ibid.). In the case of Iraq societal discrimination may have actually increased following the state's temporary legalization of homosexuality. Instances of violence against the LGBTQ+ community in Iraq surged after it was legalized in 2003 (Alizadeh 2014). This includes violence perpetuated by the Islamic State (also commonly referred to as 'ISIS' or 'ISIL'), a terrorist organization that has reportedly thrown gay men off of buildings in Mosul (Damon and Bilginsoy 2015).

There is a strong social stigma attached to sexual and gender deviation in every state in the region, but some states stand out when it comes to discrimination. Türkiye had the eighth highest rate of recorded murders against transgender people in the world with a total of twenty-three instances of homicide occurring between 2008 and 2011 (TGEU 2012). High profile murders against trans women is an ongoing problem; they have been beaten to death, attacked with acid, and sexually assaulted, but many cases go unreported (Celik 2021). Amid this violent climate President Recep Tayyip Erdoğan has denounced LGBTQ+ people and "flatly denied the existence of transgender people" altogether (Ibid.). All of these issues in the region are compounded for queer people with intersectional[107] identities (i.e. an individual belonging to two or more types of minority groups).

From a sociopolitical perspective, there is a dearth of egalitarianism with respect to homosexuality and trans identities in the region overall. In order to evaluate attitudes towards homosexuality specifically, Pew Research Center (2013) conducted a poll with an average sample size of 962 respondents

---

[107] See "Intersectionality" in Glossary for definition.

from seven MENA states and territories[108] and found that, with the exception of Sub-Saharan Africa, the MENA region is the least tolerant of homosexuality.[109] Feelings towards homosexuality are gauged with a 3-point ordinal level variable utilizing the Likert scale. The frequency distribution indicates a strong aversion towards the notion of homosexuality; 47% of Israelis, 78% of Turks, 80% of Lebanese, 93% of Palestinians, 94% of Tunisians, 95% of Egyptians, and 97% of Jordanians believe society should not accept homosexuality (Ibid.). With a mean of 83%, median of 93%, and approximate standard deviation of 17 (8 when excluding Israel) it is clear that attitudes towards homosexuality are generally negative.[110] When controlling for nominal-level variables such as age there is not much variation. An increase in age typically leads to a decrease in tolerance for homosexuality—this is the case in many regions such as Latin America, North America, and Europe—but Lebanon is the only state in the region where support among younger generations is much higher than older generations[111] (Pew Research Center 2013).

---

[108] States included in the study are Israel, Lebanon, Türkiye, the Palestinian territories, Egypt, Jordan, and Tunisia.

[109] It should be noted that this dataset contains other states, but the MENA region is singled out in this discussion in order to determine attitudes towards homosexuality in the region.

[110] Although one could technically make the case that attitudes towards homosexuality in Israel are heterogenous for the fact that a large portion (40%) believe homosexuality should be accepted, which indicates views on the matter are polarized (see Pew Research Center 2013).

[111] In Lebanon 27% of 18-29 year-olds, 17% of 30-49 year-olds, and 10% of individuals 50 years-old and up believe homosexuality should be accepted; a trend common in many other states, but not those in the MENA region (Pew Research Center 2013).

These results remain consistent with other datasets. The World Values Survey (2010-2014) measured the justifiability of homosexuality with a 10-point interval-level variable with sample sizes ranging from 1,000 to 2,131 respondents (with a mode of 1,200) and found that an average of 68.0% of MENA citizens from thirteen states[112] believe homosexuality is never justifiable (V203). In this dataset the most conservative responses came from Qatar, Tunisia, Jordan, and Morocco (with 91.7%, 87.1%, 85.6%, and 83.6% all respectively stating homosexuality is never justifiable) while the least conservative responses came from Cyprus at 36.5% and Bahrain at 42.3% (Ibid.).

In a survey conducted by Gallup, McCarthy (2014) found that citizens in most MENA states do not think their area of residence is hospitable to gays and lesbians; 62% of Tunisians, 68% of Turks, 80% of Palestinians, 81% of Lebanese, and 91% of Mauritanians[113] indicated this view. In sum, these surveys typify a regionally consistent aversion to homosexuality seeing that many individuals believe it is morally repugnant. The small percentage of individuals that are gay, lesbian, bisexual, or transgender—and the even smaller percentage of individuals who will actually opt to "come out"[114] in this region—face severe discrimination due to a strong cultural aversion to the idea of one deviating away from prominent sex and gender norms.

---

[112] The states/territories included in this dataset are Algeria, Bahrain, Cyprus, Palestine, Iraq, Jordan, Lebanon, Libya, Morocco, Qatar, Tunisia, Türkiye, and Yemen.

[113] Conversely, 49% of Israelis and 50% of Cypriots state that their area of residence is hospitable to gays and lesbians, which is quite impressive from a comparative standpoint (McCarthy 2014).

[114] See "Coming Out" in Glossary.

There is some cause for hope that attitudes are incrementally changing for the better in some states. Since the aforementioned surveys were published. An Arab Barometer survey conducted between 2018-2019 asked a total of 25,407 respondents in ten states whether or not homosexuality was acceptable; more than a quarter of Algerians (26%) answered 'Yes,' which is a positive sign. Furthermore, 21% of Moroccans now accept homosexuality compared to 79% of the population who do not (Ibid.). This indicates views towards homosexuality in Morocco are slowly trending in a positive direction when juxtaposed with the World Values Survey's dataset from 2010-2014, where 83.6% said homosexuality was never justifiable, (which is a 4.6-point swing). Attitudes towards homosexuality in Palestine have slightly improved as well, with 5% accepting homosexuality (Arab Barometer 2018-2019) compared to 95% who do not accept homosexuality. This is a 2-point swing when compared to 93% of Palestinians in 2013 that said society should reject homosexuality. The same Arab Barometer poll found that attitudes have slightly improved in Jordan and Tunisia. More recently, 93% of Jordanians and 93% of Tunisians do not find homosexuality acceptable compared to the 97% of Jordanians and 94% of Tunisians that said homosexuality was never justifiable in 2013 (see Pew 2013) That's a 4-point swing in Jordan and a 1-point swing in Tunisia (though it should be noted this increase is within the margin of error).

Unfortunately, cautious optimism is advised, because attitudes don't necessarily trend in one linear direction. For example, attitudes have seemingly regressed in Lebanon despite some political momentum to decriminalize homosexuality. Arab Barometer (2018-2019) finds that 94% of Lebanese people do not find homosexuality acceptable compared to 80% of Lebanese people in 2013 that said homosexuality was never justifiable (see Pew 2013). That's a 14-point decrease, which is significant even taking into consideration the fact that both surveys are worded differently.

An increase in negative attitudes towards LGBTQ+ people —while not necessarily a regional trend with respect to the MENA—is not unheard of, nor is it unique to Lebanon. Even in the United States, where support for same-sex marriage has reached an unprecedented high, attitudes towards transgender Americans have decreased following a wave of anti-trans legislation in Republican-controlled states in conjunction with an anti-trans media campaign by conservatives. Outright bans on gender-affirming care, restrictions on access to hormone-replacement therapy (HRT), the policing of trans Americans' bathroom usage, bans on trans women and girls in sports, fear mongering over trans identities being a "social contagion" and even hysterical accusations that China is using TikTok to turn American children trans[115] has culminated in a nationwide decrease in acceptance of trans people. By May of 2022 just 38% of respondents in a poll conducted by Pew Research Center (2022) said a person "[c]an be different from sex assigned at birth" compared to 44% of respondents who answered the same in

---

[115] This is not hyperbole. On a March 22, 2023 episode of *The Charlie Kirk Show*, Kirk and his guest, Chaya Raichik (of the notoriously anti-LGBTQ+ account 'Libs of TikTok' on Twitter), falsely claimed not only that trans identities were attributable to a "social contagion," but also suggested "Chinese Communist Party military installations are programming the algorithm to make our children more likely to be trans" (See Media Matters for America 2023 in references). This rhetoric is emblematic of the toxic environment conservatives cultivated in 2023.

2017.[116] Views towards trans people in America vary depending on the question and specific issue, but this demonstrates that attitudes towards LGBTQ+ people are volatile everywhere and may change depending on political dynamics.

The Social Climates in Morocco, Algeria, & Tunisia

Tunisia has a long reputation of being both a social and legally egalitarian state. It was the first country in North Africa to offer substantial rights to female citizens. President Habib Bourguiba liberalized the Tunisian Personal Status Code in 1956 and granted extensive rights to women upon his state's independence, which was unprecedented for the region (Lust 2013, 796).

Conversely, progress in Morocco stagnated under King Hassan II (Ibid., 664). Once King Mohammed VI inherited the throne, he reformed Morocco's moudawana (family code) in 2003 and granted women an extensive set of rights, thus putting them on par with Tunisia and making the country a bit more progressive from a legal standpoint. Lust argues that laws have become more equitable as a result of King Mohammed VI's ambitions to integrate Morocco into the world economy (665). For this reason the importance of both domestic and international legitimacy is evident to King Mohammad VI, as his willingness to modernize Morocco has been quite comprehensive. However, this does not

---

[116] Attitudes towards trans people, overall, are mixed. A strong majority of Americans (64%) favor protections for trans people from discrimination in employment or housing, but generally support discrimination when it comes to certain issues like sports and healthcare coverage (See Pew Research Center 2022).

diminish the fact that Morocco is still conservative from a social and cultural standpoint (664).

Algeria, much like Morocco, has a long history of being relatively conservative from both a societal and legal perspective (see Charrad 2001). New blatantly discriminatory family codes were codified in 1984 under President Chadli Bendjedid, which "proclaim[ed] women as minors under the law, and define[d] them as existing only in so far as they are daughters, mothers, or wives" (Salhi 2010, 27). In 2004 President Abdelaziz Bouteflika signaled that change was "imperative" (Watan 2004) and moved forward with the reformation of their family penal codes in 2005 (Marzouki 2010). Article 31 of the Algerian constitution now grants political autonomy to women (Ibid.), although they have yet to reach parity with men in many respects. Social reforms will not immediately ameliorate decades of cultural conservatism that was reinforced institutionally by discriminatory laws, but understanding family codes in these three states allows one to gauge the overall social climate of each country.

Seeing as how Tunisians have had over fifty years to acclimate to their state's liberal social status codes, one would be reasonable to deduce that this would consequentially result in more egalitarian views towards LGBTQ+ rights. Tunisians may still not be personally inclined to embrace the prospect of social or legal equality for the queer community (seeing as how Pew Research Center [2013] finds that Tunisians are the most averse to homosexuality in the region), but they could potentially be more apt to tolerate its existence than their neighbors.

In fact, Tunisia *is* comparatively more tolerant of homosexuality at least from a legal standpoint. Female homosexuality has presumably remained legal or has not been explicitly criminalized, whereas male homosexuality has been long prohibited (Itaborahy and Zhu 2014, 48). Both male and female homosexuality is unlawful in Morocco and Algeria (Ibid., 40, 30). Predictably, Tunisia is more legally indifferent to homosexuality; but in contrast, Morocco and Algeria are not. It is fairly common for the latter two states to persecute and prosecute individuals that violate anti-homosexuality laws, but irrespectively, LGBTQ+ activism is still able to thrive in both countries.

Persecution Against the Moroccan LGBTQ+ Community

The Moroccan monarchy exhibits a morally ambiguous attitude towards the notion of homosexuality, but this fact does not imply anti-homosexuality laws go unenforced or that gay and trans Moroccans are not disproportionately targeted in homophobic and transphobic acts of violence. Anti-sodomy laws are enforced quite fervently by authorities at the local levels. Legal and social persecution against the Moroccan LGBTQ+ community is not only common, but severe to the extent that it made queer activism a necessity as soon as new political resources came to fruition.

While the King has an incentive to cultivate international legitimacy and remain attentive to the growing international sentiment against homophobia, he has largely turned a blind eye to systemic homophobia perpetrated by lower level government officials. Instead of arresting gay men and women for violating Article 489—the Moroccan penal code that criminalizes homosexuality—authorities help perpetuate the facade that Morocco is "gay-friendly" by charging gay people with unrelated offensives such as prostitution or alcoholism while simultaneously being more lenient towards gay tourists (Hayoun 2014a). This is not always the case seeing that Moroccan officials have sparked international outrage in the past by jailing a gay British man in Marrakech, but such an event is out of the norm (Rawlinson 2014). Not all gay tourism is welcome, however, as a gay cruise was diverted away from a port in Casablanca after authorities prohibited it from docking (Gray 2012), but overall, authorities tolerate acts of homosexuality by foreigners insofar as their lack of action does not spark outrage among the conservative constituents of local officials, police and politicians.

Acts of homosexual intimacy are singled out in comparison to other acts deemed sexually immoral. Local police turn a blind eye to heterosexual brothels and allow pre-marital sex between opposite-sex partners to go unpunished (Ibid.). It is estimated that thousands of gay men have been imprisoned for being gay since Morocco gained independence (Harit 2013). While the aforementioned statistic is unsubstantiated, one does not have to look far to find anecdotes that speak to the prevalence of state-sanctioned homophobia. Numerous examples illustrate homophobic abuse by the state.

According to the Index on Censorship (2005) forty men and women were all simultaneously jailed for two days for suspected homosexuality, and additionally, thirteen filmmakers were sentenced to a cumulative total of thirty years in prison for filming sexually explicit videos involving gay men (Rhanem 2006). These crackdowns on homosexuality are not isolated; quite contrarily, they occur fairly frequently. Two men were jailed after being suspected of homosexuality for just sitting in their car together according to Al Arabiya News (2013). Furthermore, the U.S. Department of State (2013, Section 6) cites another case wherein three gay men were sentenced to three years imprisonment for homosexuality. Moreover, six men in Fquih Ben

Saleh were convicted of homosexuality (Hayoun 2014a). In 2015 two more men were arrested for homosexuality and convicted less than one month later in al Hoceima, which illustrates how swift the ramifications are for homosexuality (S. Roberts 2015). These instances only encapsulate cases in which LGBTQ+ individuals were actually prosecuted for violating anti-homosexuality laws. One can speculate that many more cases go unreported seeing as how gay men and women may technically be indicted for homosexual acts, but charged with an irrelevant crime in an effort to avoid international scrutiny (see Hayoun 2014a).

The most prominent case of homophobia paints a bleak picture for Morocco's LGBTQ+ community for the fact that it highlights both legal and societal persecution. Pfeiffer and Abdennebi (2008) reports that Moroccan authorities raided the house of several men thought to be guilty of allegedly participating in an illegal Sufi-esque wedding between a same-sex couple—one of which was believed to be in drag—after an online video of the event surfaced. The family of one of the men involved maintains that no wedding took place at the residence (Ibid.). Still, due to persistent coverage and sensationalization, the media may have implicitly incited violence by doxing the men involved with the making of the video by releasing their names to the public (Belonksy 2008). As a result the house where the "ceremony" took place attracted a mob of fundamentalists who rioted and ultimately destroyed the residence in its entirety according to Pfeiffer and Abdennebi. Belonksy explains that the alleged same-sex wedding video managed to amass a large following and various Moroccan media outlets capitalized on its popularity. One Moroccan newspaper, *Al Massae*, was fined €100,000 for inaccurately reporting that a judge was in attendance of the said wedding (Grew 2008). This event is only one of many publicized stories that accentuates the media's ability to exacerbate already homophobic attitudes by sensationalizing LGBTQ+ stories and vilifying the community.

The Overseas Security Advisory Council (2014) declared that Moroccan LGBTQ+ individuals encounter "a great deal of [societal] pressure and/or discrimination" in its 2014 Crime and Safety Report. The aforementioned empirical examples as well as others substantiate this point. Gay men and women have a unique challenge in Morocco. One Moroccan lesbian was physically assaulted multiple times in the same week by a disgruntled ex-boyfriend once he learned she had become involved in a romantic relationship with a woman (Hafften 2012). She did not file a police report for the fact that she anticipated her ex-boyfriend would likely retaliate by reporting her for homosexuality, which would in turn subject *her* to imprisonment instead (Ibid.). Moroccan director Mahmoud Frites incited violence against Moroccan actor Adam Lahlou (aka Adouma) by sharing a picture of him on Facebook in a head scarf (which he likely perceived as him crossdressing) and called for him to be raped, and offered to "pay money" for someone to do it (Beresford 2017). After Frites' call for violence went viral, Adouma was subsequently attacked. LGBTQ+ victims of hate-inspired violence have no legal recourse, as reporting such assaults would require them to indirectly out themselves to authorities and face prosecution.

Moroccan society is very hostile to the notion of homosexuality. Merely bringing up the matter is grounds for outrage. One member of The Party of Justice and Development alleges that public discourse on homosexuality that is perpetuated by NGOs violates the religious values of Moroccans[117] (Sidiguitiebe 2014). A BBC reporter apologized in 2023 after asking Moroccan soccer star Ghizlane Chebbak whether or not she had any gay teammates during a press conference for the Women's World Cup (Grez 2023). Members of the Moroccan press were reportedly "audibly dismayed," and Chebbak brushed the question off as "political" (Ibid.).[118] Isolated events such as seminars pertaining to LGBTQ+ issues are the subject of public outrage when they occur (Hassan Al-Ashraf 2009). Acceptance of even the smallest semblance of contemplation or discussion of homosexuality may be viewed as a tacit endorsement of it (Ibid.). The climate for the Moroccan LGBTQ+ community is undeniably toxic.

Queerphobia in Algeria

There is evidence to suggest the LGBTQ+ community in Algeria also encounters an immense degree of legal and societal discrimination, although to a lesser extent than queer Moroccans. It is still endemic nonetheless. While news stories involving arrests of the LGBTQ+ community occur less frequently in

---

[117] It should be noted that this is a rough paraphrasing of what was said seeing that the article in question was translated from French to English.

[118] The BBC reporter presumably intended to draw attention to homophobia in Morocco and how it impacts players. However, her question was deemed "inappropriate" for multiple reasons; first the subject of homosexuality is taboo in Morocco, and second, if Chebbak confirmed some of her teammates were lesbians, she would have effectively outed them and opened them up to prosecution (see Greg 2023). Thus, it was largely viewed as inappropriate from both proponents and opponents of LGBTQ+ rights, albeit for very different reasons.

Algeria, this does not imply legal persecution is not prevalent, but instead that stories surrounding LGBTQ+ issues are less sensationalized in comparison to Morocco. Numerous personal accounts and anecdotal examples demonstrate that societal discrimination could be a bit more salient in Algeria than in Morocco.

An Algerian transgender woman alleges she received multiple death threats from religious conservatives and notes that employment discrimination is a common occurrence for her (Tutton 2010). An Algerian gay rights activist, Yahia Zaidi, explains how many gays are commonly subjected to homophobic physical violence (Schweiger 2011). According to the United Nations High Commissioner for Refugees, the LGBTQ+ community faces severe familial discrimination. Honor killings against gays is a phenomenon that still takes place in Algeria when individuals feel a gay family member has disgraced the family's name (see "UNHCR" 2007). This is one of many reasons why the LGBTQ+ community is relegated to a perpetual life of secrecy since Algeria's overtly hostile social climate makes the prospect of coming out infeasible (Slimane 2010).

The Algerian LGBTQ+ community also encounters state-sponsored persecution—primarily at the local level—as is the case in Morocco (UNHCR 2007). Police often persecute and intimidate gay men and women. Yahia Zaidi was arrested for violating anti-homosexuality laws (333 and 338 of the Algerian penal code) and alleges that local authorities plagiarized his signature on a confession form that he refused to sign which professed that he was culpable for acts of homosexuality (Schweiger 2011). This is not the only case of legal maltreatment. Even an imam was sentenced to two years in jail for committing acts of homosexuality (Boudjadi 2010). In 2020 Algerian police arrested

44 students for participating in what they believed to be a "gay wedding" due to the "gay appearance" of the men involved as well as the "decorations, flowers and sweets" that were available at the event (Wakefield 2020). Just over a month later an Algerian court convicted all 44 students on charges of "'same-sex relations', 'public indecency' and 'subjecting others to harm by breaking COVID-19-related quarantine measures'" (Ibid.).

The climate for Algerian queers is dreadful, but this is no secret. There is no veil of "gay friendliness" in Algeria, which is arguably contrary to the case of Morocco. Pink News (2007) reports that a high court in London rejected a repatriation request of an effeminate Algerian man because the court feared his life would be in jeopardy if he returned home. Violence is regularly incited against the Algerian LGBTQ+ community, as its first gay magazine, *El-Shad*, alleges it received multiple death threats for merely existing (Harim 2014). Additionally Mufti Yahia, from the Algerian Ministry of Religious Affairs, implicitly advocated for the death of homosexual individuals by stating that it is what the Qur'an suggests should be done to them (Jean-Jacques 2014). This type of rhetoric is dangerous because it resonates with religious fundamentalists who aim to justify and cloak their acts of violence—and even honor killings—in a shield of legitimacy.

Bigotry Against the LGBTQ+ Community in Tunisia

While acceptance of gay and trans individuals is not the norm in Tunisia, their standard of living is much higher compared to Morocco and Algeria. This is primarily contingent on the fact that female homosexuality is not prohibited, and to boot, the enforcement of anti-homosexual laws against men is seldom (Lucas 2012). Though many gays, lesbians, bisexuals, and transgender individuals opt to stay in the closet, it is sometimes possible for them to come out to their families without facing outright rejection, and this is especially the case in more liberal households where alcohol is consumed and women go unveiled in public (Blackshaw 2012).

In spite of an increased level of social egalitarianism in Tunisia, the situation for the LGBTQ+ community was never particularly great for a number of reasons. Male homosexuality and trans identities are illegal, the collective queer community lacks legal protection from discrimination, and same-sex couples are not granted the same rights as opposite-sex couples. This did not change after democratization.

Canning (2011) reports that Ennahda, one of Tunisia's largest political parties, initially pledged to support the liberty of LGBTQ+ citizens and inferred that their platform would include support for the decriminalization of male homosexuality. However, according to Littauer (2012), Ennahda's Health Minister, Samir Dilou, spoke out against the gay community and argued democratic principles such as freedom of expression should not account for "perversion" and stated his belief that gays need medical treatment. The party subsequently adopted an anti-gay platform as a scare tactic to dissuade voters from electing parties with more secular platforms, although it is quite possible that several internal gay scandals within the party likely triggered the adoption of such a hardline stance on the matter (Ibid.).

Religiosity has surged since democratization and a discernible Salafist movement has since burgeoned (Blackshaw 2012). Seeing as how subscribers of Salafism often adhere to its homophobic tenants it is logical to speculate the extent to which this has lead to a rise in societal homophobia. Perhaps for the first time, a tourist was arrested in Tunisia for committing homosexual acts, which was unanticipated considering it is unconventional for authorities in the region to penalize tourists for homosexuality (Morgan 2015).

There is anecdotal evidence to suggest police violence against LGBTQ+ people actually increased following Tunisia's 2011 revolution. Greater freedom to politically organize lead to growth in police unionization which, in turn, made police unions a powerful political force and consequentially emboldened homophobic police officers that wanted to harass and assault queer Tunisians with impunity (Ebel 2021). Badr Baabou, a longtime Tunisian gay rights activist, was attacked by police officers while trying to report police misconduct in 2021 (Ibid.).

LGBTQ+ communities in Morocco, Algeria, and Tunisia face an inordinate amount of discrimination, hence the need for unity and political coordination among the aggregate community. However, public advocacy for queer equality in the MENA is tantamount to social suicide and potentially an incitement of violence against oneself. For this reason, political mobilization among LGBTQ+ communities in all three of these states is done in a manner that is mostly discrete and as inconspicuous as possible.

CHAPTER 3

Profiling the Relative Strength of LGBTQ+ Movements in Morocco, Algeria, & Tunisia

Lesbian, gay, bisexual, and transgender rights movements in Morocco and Algeria—two socially conservative states—are surprisingly robust. Morocco's queer rights movement is more formally organized and prominent than Algeria's; but nevertheless, both are politically active and decent at providing outreach to members of their communities. Prior to the 2011 Tunisian revolution, members of the LGBTQ+ community in Tunisia were not overtly politically active at all (with a few exceptions) until 2012, which is when restrictions on internet freedom were lifted. Given that Tunisia has historically been much more socially liberal than its Moroccan and Algerian neighbors, a Tunisian queer rights movement should have theoretically materialized not only before Morocco and Algeria's, but much sooner than it actually did. Seeing that (a) the level of freedom on the internet as well as overall access to it varies in all three of these states, and (b) that the internet has been integral to their movements, it seems plausible to attribute variation in the strength of these movements to the internet. In order to demonstrate this, it is necessary to first determine that there is, in fact, variation in the strength of queer rights movements in Morocco, Algeria, and Tunisia altogether.

The Moroccan LGBTQ+ Movement: A Pioneer in North Africa

LGBTQ+ activism in Morocco is quite prevalent. There is sufficient evidence to suggest the queer movement in Morocco has gained an ample amount of momentum to not only be categorized into the third tier of online activism, but to also be classified as a full-fledged social movement. They have flourished into a well-organized political faction with both formal and informal organizations, LGBTQ-friendly magazines, and notable gay icons (such as Abdella Taia and Hajar El Moutaouakil) to represent them and speak out on behalf of the aggregate community. In fact, the Moroccan LGBTQ+ movement may be on the cusp of advancing to the fourth tier of activism since they arguably pose a small threat to the regime's legitimacy. Their current level of international visibility is arguably high enough to induce scrutiny on the regime if they call attention to governmental abuse, which keeps the monarchy in check and prevents it from becoming *too* punitive towards queer people (which may explain its gay-friendly facade or, at best, apathy towards homosexuality). The ability of gay and trans activists to obtain straight and cis allies such as domestic pro-civil rights organizations (Hayoun 2014a) and international actors (ranging from American and British celebrities to NGOs) has allowed them to increasingly cultivate more political clout at an expeditious pace.

In 2010 King Mohammed VI did not cede to the demands of anti-gay social conservatives that petitioned him to disallow Elton John, an openly gay British musician, from performing at Morocco's annual Marwazine music festival (Ghanmi 2010). Officials from Morocco's largest Islamic party, The Party of Justice and Development, along with Islamists across the country voiced concerns with his performance and argued that permitting such an event could corrupt Moroccan youth by encouraging sexual promiscuity and alcoholism (Ibid.). The King disregarded this rhetoric and allowed the performance to take place likely in an attempt to make Morocco appear more modern (Ibid.). It is plausible to assume King Mohammed VI's decision was contingent on the fact that he did not want to draw unwelcome international scrutiny to the regime seeing as how it could be detrimental to his economic aspirations and impede his ability to establish international trade deals (Lust 2013, 665).

The King's indifference to homosexuality has put him in a unique political predicament, nevertheless. In an attempt to appease both religious conservatives and social progressives, he walks a fine line. In spite of the fact that he has yet to indicate support for   nor has he explicitly endorsed—any LGBTQ+ issue, his apathetic view has perpetuated a plethora of rumors that he himself might be gay. The search query "is king mohammed vi gay?" turns up 5,630,000 results on Google in Arabic, 430,000 results in English, and 323,000 results in French[119]. This clearly

---

[119] These results are based off the translation of the search term from English to Arabic and from English to French.

speaks to the fact that many Moroccans are highly conservative when it comes to homosexuality and that anything short of unequivocal condemnation of it will result in criticism. This is problematic for the fact that it incentivizes individuals to become unabashedly homophobic in an attempt to appear less suspicious themselves. Irrespectively, the King has allowed openly gay pop stars to return to the country.

Four years after Elton John's visit Morocco opened the doors to Ricky Martin, who gave a nod to Morocco's LGBTQ+ community during his performance by changing all female pronouns in his song lyrics to male pronouns (Wong 2014). This illustrates how Moroccan queer activists have managed to gain support from gay rights activists abroad who are willing to make statements on their behalf (though such a gesture serves as little more than symbolism). It also denotes the level of influence the LGBTQ+ movement in Morocco has amassed. The message they have conveyed to the world has been received.

Prominent lesbian Moroccan activist Hajar El Moutaouakil was one of 18 LGBTQ+ activists from multiple Arab countries that participated in a 2018 visibility campaign spearheaded by the Arab Foundation for Freedoms and Equality and Human Rights Watch (Jao 2018). The goal of the campaign was to heighten the visibility of LGBTQ+ activism in the MENA region and elevate queer stories. Hajar, for example, talked about the difficulty in coming to terms with her sexuality and explained "how authorities in Morocco play on family dynamics to intimidate activists, using 'family as a tool of repression'" (Ibid.). After gaining notoriety for her queer activism in Morocco, Hajar was forced to moved to Europe after receiving death threats (Ibid.).

Morocco's first formal gay rights organization, Kif-Kif, has existed since 2005 (Bradley 2010, 250). Kif-Kif is a pro-

LGBTQ+ advocacy organization that is headquartered in Spain with approximately fifty staff members (Ibid.). Smith (2010) reports that Kif-Kif has been directly instrumental in the creation of Morocco's first queer magazine, *Mithly* (meaning "the same as me" in English). Their next goal is to construct a "center to provide psychological support" for members of the LGBTQ+ community in Morocco, but this goal is not within reach at the moment (Association Alouen 2011). Nonetheless, they have been instrumental at fostering discussions about LGBTQ+ rights and are considered a "leader" in the Maghreb (Ibid.).

Kif-Kif has faced harassment amid growing levels of eminence. Their web domain has been hacked multiple times by anti-gay Islamic groups (Bradley, 250); still, Kif-Kif has not disbanded. Moroccan activists have proven to be resilient. Though political demonstrations are prohibited in Morocco, LGBTQ+ activists often participate in pride marches abroad, where they are safe to do so (Hayoun 2014b). LGBTQ+ activism has steadily burgeoned in Morocco since its inception. Its queer rights movement has acquired a substantial level of influence compared to other LGBTQ+ movements in the region. Their presence has, in effect, prevented the monarchy from becoming more abusive, although they have been unsuccessful at pressuring King Mohammed VI to reign in local authorities.

LGBTQ+ Activism in Algeria: Late Start, Steady Growth

Seeing as how discrimination permeates throughout Algerian society, there is undoubtedly a need for political mobilization. Besides having a magazine for LGBTQ+ people, the queer movement in Algeria has progressed to the point to also be categorized into the third tier of postmaterialist activism; however, it is arguably not on par with Morocco's LGBTQ+ movement. Nonetheless, the movement—also rooted in online activism—has grown appreciably since its emergence.

There are two prominent LGBTQ+ associations in Algeria; Alouen and Abu Nawas. Alouen is an activist organization that prioritizes social equality and advocates for decriminalization of homosexuality and the repeal of penal codes 333 and 338 (see "Association Alouen" in references). On the other hand, Abu Nawas is more outreach-oriented and provides various resources to members of the gay community such as education on safe-sex practices (see "Abu Nawas"). Both organizations specialize in political mobilization; Alouen coordinates events while Abu Nawas encourages LGBTQ+ citizens to vote (Ibid.). Additionally, there are two prominent online-exclusive LGBTQ+ magazines: *Lexo Fanzine*, a magazine tailored to lesbian issues such as increasing the visibility of women in the LGBTQ+ community, as well as *Kelmaghreb*, which focuses on issues of interest to gay men (Jean-Jacques 2014). Moreover the Algerian LGBTQ+ community participates in the International Day Against Homophobia and Transphobia (Ibid.). According to Afrol News (2010) the LGBTQ+ Facebook group, "Union des Gays et Lesbiennes en Algérie," mobilized members of the community to light thousands of candles in public in order to elevate the visibility of the LGBTQ+ community and call for the decriminalization of homosexuality.

Algerian activists have also been successful in founding 'TenTen,' the national day of celebration for LGBTQ+ individuals. Their biggest success, much like the Moroccan LGBTQ+ community, has been to gain the support of international allies who have called for a repeal of laws criminalizing homosexuality at a UN Human Rights Council event in Geneva on behalf of gay and lesbian Algerians (Jean-Jacques 2014). These savvy activists acknowledge that greater visibility and international support are necessary for them to actualize these goals. With respect to the strength of movements, Morocco and Algeria are fairly similar, but Morocco's movement is a bit stronger and may advance to the fourth tier of activism relatively soon. This is primarily due to Morocco's LGBTQ+ movement being more formerly organized and having a greater level of international visibility.

The Tunisian LGBTQ+ Movement: Nonexistent Until Democratization

It is easier to be a member of the LGBTQ+ community in Tunisia than in Morocco or Algeria, but there is still an unmistakable need for political mobilization. Nevertheless, there were virtually no signs of LGBTQ+ activism or organizing under Ben Ali's repressive authoritarian regime that were detectable to the outside world.[120] Upon his ousting, LGBTQ+ groups like the Tunisian Association for Justice and Equality (or Damj)—created by Tunisian gay rights activist Badr Baabou all the way back in 2002—made its presence known to the world. Damj is an interesting organization for the fact that it defies expectations of this book in that it was not likely birthed on the internet, nor did it have a significant presence online until the mid-2010s. Peace Insight (2021) reports, "Damj began it's [sic] work by creating safe and secure spaces for the LGBT Community in Tunisia" as

---

[120] This is due to a lack of internet freedom in Tunisia. To the extent that LGBTQ+ groups existed under Ben Ali's regime, they would have been forced to be mostly offline due to heavily restrictions on internet freedom.

well as "legal support" following a "wave" of arrests of queer Tunisians. The organization presumably operated covertly as an underground queer support network until it tried to become a legally recognized formal organization in 2009, however, it was not officially granted recognition until after the 2011 revolution (Ibid.). Since then Damj has become much more prominent, as has its founder, Badr Baabou.

One of the first pro-gay Tunisian Facebook pages to manifest following the revolution, "Kelmty - Associations Gays et Lesbiennes Tunisiens,"[121] appeared in 2012 and managed to finally surpass 1,500 likes by March 2014 and amassed over 2,500 likes nearly a year later. It currently has 3,500 likes, but became inactive as of 2016. Despite its current inactivity, Kelmty founded a website to act as a portal to their blog and various social media sites. Kelmty differs from groups like Kif-Kif and Alouen in that it does not coordinate pro-equality events or protests, but instead highlights issues that impact the Tunisian LGBTQ+ community. Moreover, a Maghreb-based online magazine, "Gayday," which covers North African gay issues, has managed to gain popularity among Tunisia's gay community; although it was not created by Tunisia's LGBTQ+ community and is instead a regional magazine that is inclusive of them (Littauer 2012).

The Huffington Post (2015) reports that, in addition to Kelmty, more informal organizations have emerged following the

---

[121] See "Kelmty - Associations Gays et Lesbiennes Tunisiens" 2015 in references.

evolution including several Facebook pages like "LGBTI[122] Tunisien" and "Decriminalization of Homosexuality in Tunisia." While the extent of LGBTQ+ activism in Tunisia was limited at the start of the movement, it quickly transcended the internet in small ways. For example, by 2015 the U.S. Department of State (2016) reports that LGBTQ+ organizations were already starting to coordinate public rallies and even a modest (albeit "discreet") pride event in Tunis (24). Additionally, several LGBTQ+ organizations quickly gained legal recognition to the chagrin of Tunisian social conservatives.

Shams was granted legal recognition in May of 2015 on the condition that it remained focused on its "declared objectives" of "defending sexual minorities," forming "support groups for young people who struggle with sexual orientation," and "raising awareness about sexually transmitted diseases" (Khlifi 2015). In other words, the association can openly advocate for support and tolerance, but cannot explicitly advocate for legal rights for queer people. Within its first year of operation, a Tunisian court punished Shams with a 30-day suspension after it was accused of advocating for gay rights, which supposedly breached its agreement to not deviate from its "declared objectives" (AWID 2016), although the suspension was reversed after Shams filed an appeal and won (Icotza 2016).

Nevertheless, the suspension was a signal to Shams that the government would keep them on a short leash; but despite legal limitations, the organization has been able to flourish nonetheless. Shams' success may hinge—at least partially—on its

---

122 The "I" in this acronym represents intersex individuals who are born with ambiguous genitalia and/or deviate genetically or biologically from binary sexes in other ways. This is an oversimplification since the "intersex" label may be applicable in other situations as well.

controversy. Khlifi reports, "the announcement caused a stir in the country" which almost certainly boosted its name recognition inadvertently and lead to the government expressing its intent to "monitor the group's activities" (Khlifi 2015). For this fact, the group faces unique restrictions most informal organizations typically do not have to worry about. Its status as a legally recognized association provides LGBTQ+ activists with a veneer of legitimacy, therefore they have an incentive to stay within the parameters of respectability imposed by the government to not jeopardize that important status.

Shams' growth has been steady since its inception. The official Shams Facebook page has more than 133,000 likes and followers.[123] In a first for Tunisia—and the Arab world—Shams' executive director, Bounded Belhedi, launched an online radio station dedicated to LGBTQ+ issues that promotes "tolerance" (Kanso 2017). Belhedi says he has received thousands of hateful messages and even threats following the launch, but remains committed to broadcasting regardless (Ibid.). Mounir Baatour, a cofounder of Shams and an attorney, announced he was running for president in 2019 in Tunisia's Liberal Party, making him "the first openly gay presidential candidate in the Muslim world" (Asmelash and Ries 2019) who says he was previously "jailed for three months for sodomy in 2013" (Cordall 2019). Although, the Tunisian Coalition for LGBTQI+ Rights, which represents queer organizations such as Chouf, Damj and Mawjoudin (and formerly Shams), distanced themselves from Baatour and Shams the year before his announcement due to tactical disagreements with

---

[123] Titled "*Shams - Pour la dépénalisation de l'homosexualité en Tunisie.*" They predominantly post in Arabic, but have some English posts to attract wider audiences.

Figure 3.1: Strength of LGBTQ Movements in Morocco, Algeria, & Tunisia

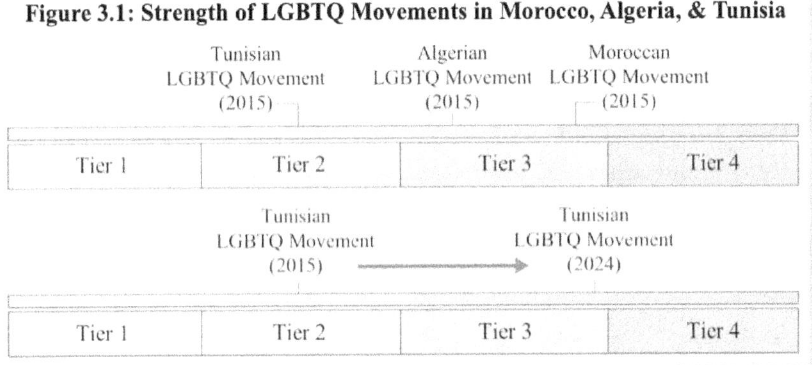

regard to "outing" homophobic politicians, sexual harassment allegations against him, as well as his call for the "total normalization" of relations with Israel (Stewart 2018). Shams accused the Tunisian Coalition for LGBTQ+ of "defamation" and suggested they were jealous of their success (Ibid.). There are reports that Shams was Tunisia's first legally recognized LGBTQ+ association, but Mawjoudin was actually granted a license to operate as a non-governmental organization in 2014 and has amassed over 19,000 likes and 21,000 followers on its Facebook page.

Like Shams, Mawjoudin does not explicitly advocate for decriminalization or legal rights for queer people; rather, it is a proponent of "justice for LGBTQI ++ individuals" and offers resources as well as legal support for queer people (See Mawjoudin 2023). Due to Mawjoudin's relatively high-profile, its leadership takes precautions to avoid harassment by only sharing their first names publicly and censoring their eyes in photographs posted to their website. Mawjoudin offers a plethora of services to LGBTQ+ Tunisians and boasts about its advocacy for queer individuals in 38 cases in 2019, 40 cases in 2020, and 19 cases in

2021 (Ibid.).[124] Mawjoudin also puts on events such as drag performances, queer art exhibits, workshops and even launched an annual queer film festival in 2018.[125] Mawjoudin, a leftist association, has also shared queer critiques of capitalism (e.g. "rainbow capitalism"), protested on behalf of Palestinians in the West Bank during Israel's evictions of Sheikh Jarrah residents in 2021, and also vocalized support for Palestinians in Gaza during Israel's 2023 and 2024 siege by sharing "Queers for Palestine" signs at rallies (see "Mawjoudin We Exist" in references).[126]

Tunisia's queer rights movement, akin to neighboring Moroccan and Algerian movements, has progressed steadily since its emergence (see Figure 3.1). At the time many LGBTQ+ groups started to materialize in Tunisia (circa 2013-ish) there were seemingly more informal organizations than formal ones. Nearly a decade later, Tunisia's LGBTQ+ movement has steadily progressed and now features multiple formal advocacy

---

[124] Not all of these cases may have involved Tunisian queer people, as Mawjoudin offers support to LGBTQ+ citizens in other countries as well (See Mawjoudin 2023 in references).

[125] Mawjoudin regularly shares photos of their activity and events on their Facebook page (see Mawjoudin We Exist" in references).

[126] LGBTQ+ participation in global pro-Palestine marches in late 2023 got a surprising amount of attention after signs reading "Queers for Palestine" at various rallies went viral. Israel's official Twitter account even shared a skit satirizing queer support for Palestinian human rights with jokes about 'H' being added to the LGBT acronym for 'Hamas.' Support for Gazans was disingenuously conflated with support for Hamas militants in an effort to downplay the deaths of civilians. Thus, the "Queers for Palestine" signs at protests became a target of ridicule by Israel's defenders who attempted to frame them as ignorant, self-hating queers who advocated for homophobic Hamas militants who were hostile towards LGBTQ+ people.

organizations that are noteworthy. Between 2013 and 2023, the strength of Tunisia's LGBTQ+ movement has gradually increased from mid Tier 2 to high Tier 3, even surpassing Morocco's LGBTQ+ movement despite its substantial head start (see Figure 3.1). But even though queer activists in Tunisia hit the ground running, why did they have such a late start? Why did LGBTQ+ activism proliferate in authoritarian Morocco and Algeria, but not in pre-revolutionary Tunisia? What political opportunities would make the development of queer rights movements possible? A literature review of existing theories on what catalyzes social movements will be discussed in the following chapter.

CHAPTER 4

Social Movement Theories

A Tunisian queer rights movement was virtually nonexistent until the 2011 revolution, after Tunisia temporarily became a democracy.[127] Contrarily, fairly robust LGBTQ+ movements have existed in Morocco and Algeria since the mid and late 2000s, respectively. This implies the emergence of these movements is attributable to a particular causal factor that was not present in Tunisia until after it democratized. Therefore it will prove fruitful to evaluate theoretical explanations in existing literature to determine which factors are most conducive to the

---

[127] Democracy in Tunisia has since declined following the reversal of democratic reforms by President Kaïs Saïed. He was elected in 2019 after capitalizing on widespread dissatisfaction with democracy and subsequently consolidated power after the COVID pandemic created a political crisis for the country. After Tunisians voted in favor of a referendum allowing him to form a new constitution, Saïed drastically strengthened the presidency and stripped the judicial and legislative branches of power (see BBC 2024 in the references).

emergence of new social movements and gauge whether they are relevant to the aforesaid cases.

In order to identify casual explanations for the emergence of social movements, it is necessary to first define them. McCarthy and Zald (1977) define social movements as "a set of opinions and beliefs in a population which represents preferences for changing some elements of the social structure and/or reward distribution of a society" (1217-8). Tilly (2004) cites three components that are fundamental to social movements. First, social movements involve an "organized public effort" (Ibid., 3) that takes shape as a *"campaign* [which] extends beyond any single event" (4). Second, Tilly argues social movements necessitate the building of coalitions, "public meetings, solemn processions, vigils, rallies, demonstrations, petition drives, statements to and in the public media, and pamphleteering" (3). Finally, members of social movements should exert four characteristics that Tilly refers to as "WUNC: worthiness, unity, numbers, and commitment" (4). Melucci (1996) states that individuals within these movements seek to communicate the fact that they have poor standing in society and aim to adjust "cultural codes" to the betterment of their group (9).

Theory of Relative Deprivation and Moral Protests

There is no paucity of theoretical explanations when it comes to causal factors for political activism, particularly with respect to social movements. However, many theories fail to account for micro acts of social activism or smaller movements and instead focus on more broad macro social movements, namely revolutions whereby dissatisfaction due to governmental or economic factors is widespread. For example, Davies (1962) cites the theory of relative deprivation as an explanation for social movements. He argues that when abrupt stoppages of economic development occurs after lengthy periods of economic growth the overall "mood [of society] becomes revolutionary" (5). There is, nevertheless, attention applied to activism surrounding issues of public morality too. Jasper discusses the concept of moral protests; a form of collective action against governmental or societal acts of injustice, ranging from anti-war protests to pro-equality civil rights movements (1997, 3).

Resource Mobilization Theory & New Social Movement Theory

The emergence of social movements is widely attributed to resource mobilization theory, which is a dominate theory in social movement research (Buechler 1995). Resource mobilization theory posits that activists will mobilize once political resources surface; that is, when new opportunities for collective action manifest (e.g. a larger number of disenchanted individuals feel as though they have something to gain from protesting, organizations develop, new proxies for mobilization emerge, and/or monetary resources become available), this fosters conditions that are conducive to political mobilization seeing that it is now feasible (Reger and Dugan 2001, 337). Conversely, new social movement theory contends that social movements may materialize when dissatisfied actors aim to improve their "quality" of life and coalesce around a group identity their activism is linked to inextricably (Ibid.). Buechler states, "some new social movement theorists emphasize the role of postmaterialist values in much contemporary collective action, as opposed to conflicts over material resources" (1995, 442).

Of these two paradigms, resource mobilization theory is the most suitable when accounting for LGBTQ+ movements in authoritarian regimes. New social movement theory is cogent, but dissatisfaction alone will not likely suffice as a catalyst for queer rights movements since individuals must be *able* to engage in activism in the first place. New social movement theory lacks an important ceteris paribus condition: access to a new political resource that makes mobilization possible. The internet is the new political resource that makes queer activism in authoritarian regimes possible because it diminishes the costs of engaging in political activism. Availability of more discrete and covert options for political protests draws people to the movement since rational actors will be disinclined to engage in activism if it will further jeopardize their standing in society.

There is one reason why social movement theory is probably inapplicable to LGBTQ+ activism in authoritarian regimes: it cannot explain why queer rights movements do not exist in states where LGBTQ+ communities share common identities formed by collective marginalization. These conditions should have, according to social movement theory, fostered a common identity strong enough to catalyze queer movements in many states; however, not all states have queer movements despite the existence of shared identities among LGBTQ+ communities. This suggests a collective identity is not sufficient to catalyze queer movements, which undercuts the utility of social movement theory.

Both paradigms have faults. When it comes to resource mobilization theory, it neglects the role of identity politics in the emergence of social movements, whereas new social movement theory overemphasizes identity politics and omits the importance of new political opportunities. New social movement theory's identity thesis is compelling, but resource mobilization theory's political opportunity thesis is more pertinent given the evidence for what catalyzed LGBTQ+ movements in North Africa (provided in Chapter 6). Members of the LGBTQ+ community may *want* to mobilize due to shared histories, identities, and goals, but are unable to do so in hostile autocracies. This implies new social movement theory may be more applicable to LGBTQ+ movements in democracies. Resource mobilization theory's emphasis on political opportunities is more fitting for LGBTQ+ movements in authoritarian regimes since it presupposes that individuals with shared identities already want to engage in activism, but will refrain from doing so until they have the *ability* to, which will be determined by the level of access they have to the internet.

Modernization Theory

Modernization theory implies the emergence of queer rights movements will be contingent on society's adoption of more modern views, which is dependent on a state's level of economic development. Marks (2009) explains,

> *as societies develop they become more open, socioeconomic achievements become less tied to social background and other ascribed characteristics, and education becomes more crucial to socioeconomic outcomes. [...] Social background becomes less important and social attainment becomes more universalistic (918).*

As education becomes more salient to individuals, their views towards other issues gradually changes and becomes more modern and egalitarian, particularly with respect to issues concerning social equality, ranging from "increasing equality of opportunity in education" to "prohibiting discriminatory practices" (Ibid.). As a result of the adoption of these values, movements for these [postmaterialist] causes will begin to materialize, including queer rights movements. The theory itself is highly influential in fields within sociology and political science, but holds only a minimal level of explanatory power when it comes to LGBTQ+ movements in non-democratic regimes seeing that they have already emerged in many regimes that have not yet undergone economic industrialization or diversification.

Additional Hypotheses

Academic explanations for the development of queer rights movements in developing countries and/or authoritarian regimes are scarce. Nonetheless, there is one by M. Roberts (1995) that is eloquent. He argues that a high prevalence of HIV/AIDS—a crisis which disproportionately impacts gay and bisexual men—could catalyze gay rights activism. Gay rights groups in India, Jamaica, and Malaysia organized specifically to combat the spread of HIV and AIDS within their communities by offering treatment and education for safe-sex practices (254). He contends that an Ecuadorian gay rights group formed solely as a response to the HIV/AIDS pandemic (256). In Mexico the Grupo Orgullo Homosexual de Liberacion, made it one of their foremost concerns in spite of the fact that their formation was not premised on the idea of HIV/AIDS mitigation (Ibid.). M. Roberts writes, "the role that gay identification and gay community development plays in reducing risk behavior […] among gays cannot be underestimated" (260). The application of this hypothesis, however, is limited.

There are three main problems with the aforesaid hypothesis; all of which indicate that it may be inapplicable to LGBTQ+ activism in the Middle Eastern and North African region. First, the prevalence of HIV/AIDS is not unique to gay communities in many developing countries, especially African states. There is a high prevalence of HIV/AIDS among both heterosexuals and homosexuals in Uganda, for example, yet a large gay rights movement still exists (Kuhanen 2008). Many Sub-Saharan African states have high rates of HIV/AIDS among their entire populations, therefore mobilization within gay communities solely to combat the spread of HIV/AIDS seems redundant (if not unnecessary) unless there is a significant statistical variation in infection rates between homosexuals and heterosexuals. Second, the prevalence of HIV/AIDS in the MENA region is comparatively low; it is less than 1% in every state in the region (CIA World Factbook 2014c). Third, this hypothesis applies only to gay and bisexual men and not women. This is problematic because if HIV/AIDS were more prevalent among gay men and could catalyze activism, then one would expect a lack of participation among lesbians and bisexual women, but that is not the reality seeing that they actively participate in LGBTQ+ activism in the MENA. Such a hypothesis is well-reasoned, but likely too outdated to apply to LGBTQ+ rights movements in the MENA.

Explanations of Catalyzing Factors That Are Exclusive to the MENA Region

Most of the aforementioned theories and arguments demonstrate how and why movements formulate in a more general sense; that is, they apply to many types of movements across a broad range of regime types throughout the world. Competing theoretical perspectives and LGBTQ-specific arguments are valuable, but it is also necessary to explore catalyzing factors for grass roots mobilization that are exclusive to the Middle Eastern and North African region.

The adoption of free market-oriented neoliberal policies and globalization has contributed to a decline of the middle class in a plethora of states in the Arab world (Bayat 2002, 2). Widespread socioeconomic disenfranchisement in politically restrictive regimes has forced innovation among grass roots activists. Bayat argues sociopolitical activism—mostly in Egypt and Iran—manifests in the form of "quiet encroachment," a type of pseudo-movement wherein "direct" action is taken by activists in that they "acquire the basic necessities of their lives (land for shelter, urban collective consumption, informal jobs, business opportunities) in a quiet and unassuming, illegal fashion" (3). For example, citizens will power their shelters by stealing electricity from "municipal power poles" or illegally extend "water pipes to their domiciles" to avoid paying for water (20).

Quiet encroachment may not be politically motivated, but it has indirect political implications. Bayet refers to it as "everyday resistance" since these acts of civil disobedience cost states money (19-20). Socioeconomically disadvantaged individuals in these states are barred from participating in demonstrations, so as a means of procuring basic necessities, they take it upon themselves to obtain them unilaterally as opposed to pressuring the government to provide them. Bayat writes, "informal and often uncharged use of collective services leaves governments little choice but selectively to integrate the informal settlements, hoping to commit the residents to pay for services they have thus far used illegally" (21).

Alternately, deliberate acts of civil disobedience such as ad hoc outbreaks of riots and mass protests may be triggered by particular events (Bayat 2000). This is demonstrated by the 1980s riots that transpired throughout the region (Ibid., 5). In Morocco and Tunisia, reductions in various government subsidies catalyzed mass protests; in Algeria citizens rioted due to a rise in the cost of living (Ibid.).

More formally organized political activism in the MENA region often occurs through proxies such as nongovernmental organizations (NGOs) or labor unions (Bayat 2000). Akin to the Western world, labor unions in the MENA—though functionally limited—have been instrumental in organizing strikes and protests due to "distributive issues and unjust labor practices" (7). Similarly, NGOs have been somewhat useful to the extent that their "headquarters also act as a place of sociability, where local poor families can gather outside their homes to associate with other poor" (21). This can be useful for organizing purposes and also to build solidarity among the socioeconomically disadvantaged, but many NGOs have a more charitable character and mostly use resources to maintain social safety nets for the poor (22). Bayat contends that this is primarily due to a love-hate relationship between NGOs and states. NGOs are unable to bolster grass roots efforts because "surveillance poses a real obstacle to the autonomous and healthy operation" of their facilities (23).

It is also the case that activism begins at mosques. Muslim groups (such as the Muslim Brotherhood) have amassed tremendous amounts of political power. Islamic-oriented social movements are able to emerge and thrive due to funding from both subscribers of Islam as well as "Muslim businesses," thus allowing them to not only monetarily assist the poor by distributing basic necessities to impoverished Muslim communities, but also to become politically active in order to improve living conditions for other Muslims (16). This can pressure governments to act as if they, in effect, are forced to directly compete with these organizations for citizens' allegiance. Bayat explains that the Egyptian government enacted "measures to upgrade slums and squatter areas" in Cairo because Islamic groups had essentially established proxy governments over territories where citizens relied on their goods and services (Ibid.).

Though social movement organizations (SMOs) in the Middle East and North Africa often assumes the forms of labor unions, NGOs, and Islamic groups, their existence is not dependent on them altogether. Bayat explains, "urban grassroots groups may find that the community or neighborhood offers a sense of common identity and a ground for collective action" (9). Community activism materializes when a united group coalesces to gain power over issues that impacts them. Bayat explains how citizens have come together to protest the pollution that disproportionately affects their community, or how they have combined resources to lobby politicians (10). Solidarity among communities and the ability of citizens to unite around a common cause is a trend that is typically responsible for catalyzing movements not only in the MENA region, but elsewhere too. Though members of the LGBTQ+ community have reasons to unite around their common cause, none of these MENA-specific explanations are applicable to the rise of queer activism in the region, as they are in line with the new social movement theory school of thought, which is not suitable for the study of LGBTQ+ movements in authoritarian regimes.

The Cruciality of the Internet to Queer Rights Activism

Unlike movements motivated by economic factors, members of the lesbian, gay, bisexual, and transgender community face unique obstacles since they are loathed by governments and societies in the MENA. Their ability to forge movements will be entirely contingent upon one fundamental resource for the time being: the internet. This may not be the case for other types of movements, hence the multitude of explanations for their existence, but LGBTQ+ activism is distinct. Homosexuality and gender identity deviations are considered social taboo in every state in the region.[128] Their cause is simply too controversial for public demonstrations to occur.

Muslim-majority countries are generally more socially conservative, albeit to varying degrees. Cultural conservatism is often imposed and reinforced by state institutions. The idea of homosexuality and gender deviation is widely believed to be haram; that is, it runs contrary to the teachings of Islam, but muslims are not a monolith. Not all Muslims interpret the Qur'an or Hadith in a homophobic way, as is the case with adherents of other Abrahamic religions. Nonetheless, social conservatism is still very prevalent throughout the region. LGBTQ+ communities in this region cannot initiate mass protests, nor can they peacefully demonstrate for three reasons; (i) they comprise very small portions of the populations of each state, and (ii) doing so will result in immediate retaliation due to the highly conservative and religious nature of society, and (iii) public admittance of one's non-heterosexual or non-cisgender identity equates to a confession of guilt due to the illegality of these identities. For the fact that

---

[128] Although Iran is an exception with respect to gender identity.

they lack both numbers, social acceptance, and legal protection it is not feasible for them to engage in activism unless it is rooted in the online realm.

In the event LGBTQ+ advocates held a public demonstration, they would likely face severe repercussions in most MENA states; verbal harassment, physical assault, and could even be killed in more conservative regions. Inevitably, they would also be ostracized by peers, fired from their jobs, and arrested (seeing as how they are implicitly admitting to violating legal prohibitions against homosexuality). If the goal is to get their voices heard and pressure their governments to decriminalize homosexuality, it is *pivotal* that their activism be executed exclusively online, otherwise they will have to travel abroad to participate in other states' pride marches. However, due to the global nature of more visible annual pride parades, they would be competing with many other states' LGBTQ+ movements for press attention.

There are, of course, exceptions to this unwritten rule. Lebanon is unique in comparison with other states in that its LGBTQ+ community has participated in actual domestic public protests in front of governmental buildings, many of which have occurred in front of the Ministry of Justice in Beirut (Littaurer 2013; Amand 2012). One notable demonstration occurred due to outrage over six gay and trans individuals being detained for going to a pro-LGBTQ+ club (Littauer 2013) and another was in response to legislation mandating the use of "anal probe" tests administered exclusively to men in order to "test" them for homosexuality (Amand 2012). Additionally, nearly 200 individuals gathered in Sodeco to advocate equality for the Lebanese LGBTQ+ community (Achi 2009). Had these protests occurred in any other MENA states (excluding Israel, Türkiye and

Cyprus) swift retaliation from the state would ensue, or rather, a violent counter-protest could erupt.

Since the internet is integral to queer MENA activists, out of all the theories and arguments examined, resource mobilization theory is best able to explain the emergence of LGBTQ+ movements in MENA authoritarian regimes for two reasons. First, it is premised on the notion that the materialization of social movements is contingent on new political opportunities that make mobilization practicable. Second, the arrival of the internet—the crème de la crème of political opportunities for marginalized groups—coincides with the emergence of LGBTQ+ movements across the region in terms of timing. The cruciality of the internet to queer activism is illustrated by the fact that the Moroccan, Algerian, and Tunisian queer rights movements all had online geneses.[129] Domestic queer activism in all three states is extremely rare, and when it does occur it is typically small in scale and minimally disruptive unless it takes place online.

---

[129] It is important to note one outlier is the early existence of the Tunisian organization Damj, which was formed by Badr Baabou in 2002 (see Peace Insight 2021 in references). It was initially less politically-oriented and primarily focused on discrete outreach to community members. Informal, underground organizations like Damj exist throughout the region, but go purposefully undetected for obvious reasons. While these types of organizations may have political goals, they do not take overtly political action(s) like more traditional social movement organizations. They can, however, develop into full-fledged movement organizations once new political opportunities emerge, as was the case with Damj. Though Damj existed before Tunisians had freedom on the internet, it used its new-fangled internet freedom to augment its capabilities. Internet freedom in post-revolutionary Tunisia allowed more queer-oriented movements to organically flourish into what could quickly be described as a robust social movement. Although one organization alone is not tantamount to a movement; therefore it is still accurate to assert that Tunisia's queer movement, collectively speaking, was born online. Nevertheless, homage must be paid to Damj.

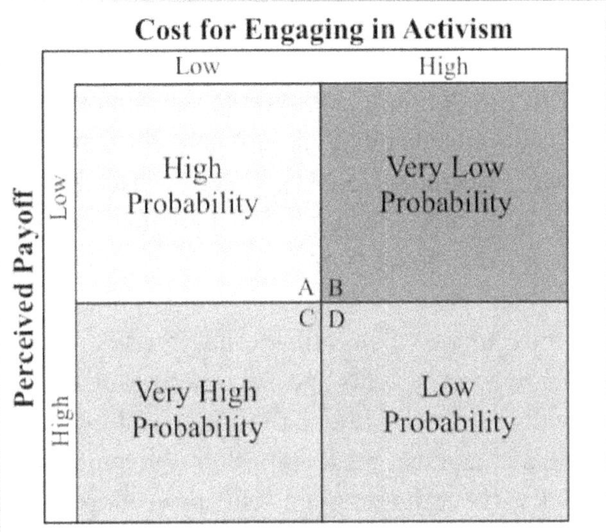

Figure 4.1: Probability for Activism

In effect, LGBTQ+ activists have two options: (a) participate in public activism abroad, or (b) engage in domestic activism almost exclusively online. Tunisian and Algerian activists opted for the latter while Moroccan activists engaged in the former. The strength of the Moroccan LGBTQ+ movement in comparison with its neighbors was much stronger in the '00s and most of the '10s, and to boot, they have existed longer, which gave them more time to acquire funds and visibility.

The internet is essential to queer activism primarily due to its capacity to lower the costs and reduce barriers for actors aiming to engage in it. If the barriers to entry for disadvantaged groups are low, one has an incentive to engage in activism to attain a higher social status. This can be explained by contrasting the costs of engaging in activism with the perceived payoff. If a group is not vulnerable and the perceived payoff is low, there will be no incentives to mobilize. Queer citizens are very vulnerable, and due to high costs, they likely predict a low payoff for engaging in activism without anonymity. The internet virtually eliminates the costs of engaging in activism, thus increasing the probability it will transpire (LGBTQ+ activism can be mapped onto quadrants A and C on Figure 4.1 if internet access is adequate). This is why queer rights movements can now emerge in authoritarian regimes.

Other movements also utilize the internet for political mobilization, but worker's rights and environmentalist movements *could* theoretically survive without the internet. Few individuals would discriminate against these types of movements because there are collective benefits entailed with protection of worker's rights or the environment. That is not the case when it comes to homosexuality and gender identity. People perceive their existence as a threat to society. For this reason, a lack of internet access makes political mobilization of the LGBTQ+ community virtually impossible due to high costs and a low payoff.

CHAPTER 5

Hypotheses Regarding LGBTQ+ Movements

There are three factors that potentially explain why a queer rights movement emerged in Morocco and Algeria, but not in Tunisia until after its democratic transition: (i) variation in internet access between states, (ii) differences in degrees of governmental, societal, and/or media discrimination, and (iii) increased political liberalization in Morocco and Algeria, but not Tunisia. One of the following three hypotheses may explain variation in the aforementioned three cases, and more broadly, explain the existence of queer rights movements in authoritarian regimes in the MENA altogether:

- **H_1: The Internet Mobilization Hypothesis** - Once citizens from marginalized groups gain sufficient access to the internet—due to increased internet penetration, the expansion of broadband infrastructure, and greater availability of smartphones—and can use it freely, they will utilize it as a tool to politically organize and fight back against government and/or societal persecution and repression. I speculate that this hypothesis will be most apt at explaining why LGBTQ+ movements exist in authoritarian regimes because resource mobilization theory contends that new political opportunities are required for the materialization of new movements. The internet is perhaps the *sole* medium in which LGBTQ+ activism is able to exist in the MENA, therefore it presents a political opportunity that makes this type of activism possible.

- **H_2: The Social Blowback Hypothesis** - When a disadvantaged group encounters a surge of persecution —regardless if the source of bias comes from the government, the media, or other members of society— the aforementioned group will mobilize in order to temporarily push back against this injustice with an episode of activism in response. If episodes of persecution increase in frequency and/or severity, the sporadic episodes of activism could become more persistent and ultimately transform into a sustained movement. This is a well-reasoned hypothesis, however, it seems more fitting for LGBTQ+ activism in democratic regimes, as it presupposes (a) barriers to the emergence of new social movements are already diminished, and (b) that a sufficient degree of repression is all that is required to catalyze a queer rights movement, but if that were the case nearly every state in the world would have a sizable LGBTQ+ movement seeing that episodes of persecution against the queer community are very common in most states.

- **H₃: The Political Liberalization Hypothesis -** More robust authoritarian regimes may aim to cultivate both domestic and international legitimacy and extend their longevity by allowing for greater levels of political participation. This may involve loosening prohibitions on public demonstrations and allowing opposition parties and other previously repressed political factions to form by holding elections for particular government offices or by facilitating greater inclusion of women and minority groups in legislatures by adopting gender quotas or reserved seats. This will result in the emergence of a plethora of new movements. By doing this the state, in effect, only pays lip service to the idea of pluralism, but it still facilitates the formation of new movements that would not otherwise exist. This hypothesis is likely a practicable explanation for the emergence of many social movements across the MENA region, but not queer rights movements. Political liberalization will be valuable to many groups, but it will not ameliorate the stigmatization of gay and trans people's existence, therefore queer rights movements may still not materialize unless they are able to mobilize in a manner that is discrete and protects their identities.

I expect that the internet mobilization hypothesis will be most able to explain why LGBTQ+ movements emerge in Middle Eastern and North African authoritarian regimes. The internet mobilization hypothesis can anticipate not only which states these movements will likely take place in, but also the overall strength of these movements. I speculate that one should be able to predict both the existence and size of a state's LGBTQ+ movement based solely on a comprehensive evaluation of internet penetration rates as well as internet freedom. Nonetheless, the other two aforementioned hypotheses could partially account for the existence of LGBTQ+ movements as well. Given this possibility, I will highlight my reasoning for why all three of these hypotheses could yield at least some explanatory value.

The Internet Mobilization Hypothesis

The internet allows for political mobilization that is anonymous and inconspicuous. It minimizes the threat of legal or physical retaliation against the group for speaking out. It also lowers both costs and barriers to engaging in activism, and for this reason, it is an invaluable political tool that LGBTQ+ rights advocates can utilize in order to stake their claim in politics. Internet access as well as internet freedom has recently become more widely available in the MENA region, therefore it seems inherently logical to attribute the rise of queer rights movements to the internet.

In comparison to the Western world the Middle East and North Africa had lower internet penetration rates for much of the 2010s, but that has changed in the 2020s. The rate of internet usage[130] (see Table 5.1) in 2014 ranged from 1% in Iraq to 61% in the United Arab Emirates with a regional average of 26% (see

---

[130] Internet penetration is calculated by converting the ratio of "internet users : total population" into a percentage using internet usage data from CIA World Factbook (2014a) and population size statistics from CIA World Factbook (2014b). The latest IPR rates are automatically calculated by Data Reportal (2020) and CIA World Factbook (2022).

CIA World Factbook 2014a; 2014b). Less than a decade later internet access increased to 60% and 100% in Iraq and the United Arab Emirates, respectively (see CIA World Facebook 2022). A majority of the populations in 18 states now have internet access, as Table 5.1 demonstrates.

In some circumstances governments may undercut the utility of internet access by implementing censorship laws. Amid growing pro-democracy protests in Algeria in 2011, President Abdelaziz Boutifleka blocked internet access for many users; numerous citizens reported that their Facebook accounts had been deleted altogether (Ramdani 2011). This is not the norm in Algeria, however. Moroccans and Algerians have enjoyed a substantial degree of freedom on the internet, whereas internet censorship was prevalent for Tunisians under Ben Ali's regime (see Freedom House 2011; Ibid. 2014; OpenNet Initiative 2009a; Ibid. 2009b). Morocco, a state with a sizable queer rights movement with a high level of visibility and influence, had a substantial rate of internet usage of 40.1% by 2014 (see Table 5.1) as well a high degree of internet freedom (OpenNet Initiative 2009b). The existence of a large Moroccan LGBTQ+ movement is consistent with the internet mobilization hypothesis bearing in mind the aforementioned internet statistics. Since LGBTQ+ movements in all three of these states emerged online—and still predominantly exist online—the internet mobilization hypothesis is likely capable of explaining the existence of these movements and why they vary in strength.

The Social Blowback Hypothesis

Blowback is a term that is not necessarily rooted in social activism, nor has it previously had academic underpinnings. It is a term coined by the U.S. Central Intelligence Agency to explain the repercussions of American militarism in the Middle East (Bergen and Reynolds 2005). Blowback is one consequence of U.S. militarism in states such as Afghanistan and Iraq. Airstrikes and the use of drones against terrorist groups such as Al Qaeda and ISIS may also result in civilian deaths which could potentially lead to further radicalization of moderate individuals in the region that would not have otherwise joined jihadist movements (Goodman 2013). Blowback is, in essence, a retaliatory response either from individuals that knew someone who became victims of U.S. aggression or from individuals that feel the U.S. is waging a "war on Islam" (Ibid.). An example is the Sunni rebellion that was triggered by the U.S. government's decision to cleanse the Iraqi government of Saddam Hussein's Ba'athist party, which ultimately lead to a civil war between Shias and Sunnis once the new Shia government began to disenfranchise Sunnis.

The blowback theory can be modified to fit sociopolitical settings. Reengineering it to explain why movements for postmaterialist causes emerge can be done in the following manner: if a government subjects a particular group of individuals to an episode of extreme persecution, that group might push back with a retaliatory response (i.e. protesting) against these acts of repression, thus spawning a brief period of activism that could ultimately result in a sustained movement. There are numerous empirical and historical examples that are illustrative of "social" blowback. The birth of the American LGBTQ+ movement surfaced due to the culmination of a months-long episode of legal persecution from the U.S. government (Falk 2014). A police raid on the Stonewall Inn gay bar in 1969 lead to social blowback in the form of a riot led by two transgender women of color, Marsha P. Johnson and Sylvia Rivera (now credited as the pioneers of the modern LGBTQ+ movement). Once the demonstrations dissipated the movement for queer equality remained. Falk writes, "the demonstrations in the days after, became a rallying cry to fight back against the force used against the patrons of the bar that night." If blowback against governmental marginalization catalyzed the American LGBTQ+ rights movement, it should, in theory, be applicable elsewhere.

David Bahati, a member of the Ugandan parliament who introduced the infamous 'kill the gays'[131] bill in the 2010s, which sought to make homosexuality punishable by death, may be responsible for spawning a wave of queer activism seeing as how LGBTQ+ Ugandans were compelled to mobilize politically in order to prevent the bill from being codified; but President Musevini ultimately signed a less harsh—albeit still draconian—version into law that made homosexuality punishable by life in prison (Karimi and Thompson 2014). In 2023 President Museveni passed what was widely referred to as "one of the world's toughest anti-gay laws" that doubled-down on life imprisonment for homosexuality and made "aggravated homosexuality" punishable by death (Northam & Athumani 2023). Things have gotten progressively worse for queer people in Uganda, but the community has never stopped resisting government oppression. After the government cracked down on homosexuality in the early 2010s, queer rights activism in Uganda has become more prevalent. The Ugandan Kuchu[132] (meaning "gay") community created and published their own magazine (Merrill 2015), held

---

[131] This quickly became the colloquial name for Bahati's legislation by queer activists after it sparked international outrage.

[132] Kuchu is a label gay Ugandans attribute to themselves.

small pride marches (Muhumuza 2014), and the movement has birthed prominent Kuchu activists like David Kato, who managed to garner a substantial amount of international fame for his LGBTQ+ activism prior to his death (Gettleman 2011). Is the Ugandan government's persecution what caused Uganda's pro-kuchu movement to materialize? This seems questionable.

Episodes of persecution from the media or social discrimination may also warrant brief periods of retaliatory activism. This is because the media are a powerful institution. They are both socially and psychologically influential on multiple levels. Media has the capacity to prime individuals and influence their standards of judgment by using a variety of manipulative strategies (see Iyengar, Peters, and Kinder 1993; McCombs 2004; Palau and Davesa 2013; Miles 2013). Moreover, media institutions in the MENA are often complicit with governmental persecution of marginalized groups. The media may cause social blowback by vilifying disadvantaged groups and further contributing to their persecution by encouraging societal homophobia. "EXPOSED!" was the headline of Ugandan's tabloid newspaper, Red Pepper, a media organization that published lists containing names and photographs of individuals that were either gay or lesbian, or suspected of being gay (Abedine and Landau 2014). This publication reinforced the need for political mobilization of Uganda's kuchu community, but once again, it is still questionable whether a direct line can be drawn between this persecution and the emergence of Uganda's pro-kuchu movement.

The Political Liberalization Hypothesis

Extraordinarily repressive regimes will not likely foster environments conducive to the augmentation of many types of movements. As a result semi-democratic, illiberal, and to a lesser extent anocratic regimes will be more inclined to allow activists to protest as a means of cultivating both domestic and international legitimacy even if a government is not sympathetic to a group's predicament. Allowing individuals to partake in protests will signal to citizens and external observers that they embrace pluralism. Seeing as how the barriers to entry for activists will be lower in these regimes, movements may materialize because, as rational actors, members of disadvantaged groups will have nothing to lose if they are already persecuted and anticipate a minimal payoff by engaging in political activism.

Though the expansion of political participation will not allow new political parties and social movements to obtain much political power, they do still arise nonetheless. With respect to the three main cases in this book, Tunisia did not undergo political liberalization under Ben Ali, whereas both Morocco and Algeria have, albeit incrementally. Therefore it must be determined whether LGBTQ+ movements emerged in Morocco and Algeria as a direct result of these changes, because admittedly, an underlying level of freedom *is* required in order for LGBTQ+ movements to exist in these countries, but whether gradual political liberalization over decades can catalyze queer rights movements—which have augmented since their inception—seems questionable. These questions will be addressed in the following chapter.

Table 5.1: Internet Penetration in the Middle East and North Africa

Algeria	Bahrain	Cyprus	Egypt	Iran	Iraq	Israel
12.1% 4.7M (2014)	31.9% 419,500 (2014)	37% 433,900 (2014)	23.2% 20.14M (2014)	10.7% 8.2M (2014)	1% 325,900 (2014)	57.9% 4.5M (2014)
63% 27.6M (2020)	100% 170,200 (2020)	91% 1.1M (2020)	72% 73.7 (2020)	84% 76.6 (2020)	60% 24.1M (2020)	90% 8.3M (2020)
Jordan	**Kuwait**	**Lebanon**	**Libya**	**Morocco**	**Oman**	**Palestine**
20.7% 1.6M (2014)	40.1% 1.1M (2014)	17% 1M (2014)	5.7% 353,900 (2014)	40.1% 13.2M (2014)	45.5 1.47M (2014)	30.3% 1.38M (2014)
67% 6.8M (2019)	99% 4.2M (2020)	84% 6.8M (2020)	22% 1.5M (2019)	84% 31M (2020)	95% 4.9M (2020)	64% 3.25M (2020)
Qatar	**S. A.**	**Syria**	**Tunisia**	**Türkiye**	**U.A.E.**	**Yemen**
26.6% 563,800 (2014)	35.7% 9.77M (2014)	24.9% 4.47M (2014)	32% 3.5M (2014)	33.4% 27.2M (2014)	61.3% 3.45M (2014)	9% 2.35M (2014)
100% 2.9M (2020)	98% 34.1M (2020)	36% 6.3M (2020)	72% 8.5M (2020)	78% 65.8M (2020)	100% 9.9M (2020)	27% 7.9M (2019)

Source: CIA World Factbook 2014a; 2014b, 2022 and Data Reportal 2020.
Note: Numbers below percentages are the total number of internet users.
Mauritania was excluded from the table due to space restraints. Its penetration was 2.1% (Pop. 3,516,806) in 2014 and 41% (Pop. 1,900,000) in 2020. Numbers are rounded to the nearest 100,000. Palestine's 2020 numbers come from Data Reportal (2020), although data from the West Bank and Gaza is aggregated.

CHAPTER 6

Variation in the Strength of Movements

I use a most similar systems research design (MSSD) to assess variation in the strength of movements between Morocco, Algeria, and Tunisia. A most similar systems design (see Charrad's 2001) is a qualitative research methodology that controls for independent variables that may explain variation in the dependent variable through case selection. Given that all three of the selected states share cultural, religious, ethnic, racial, and linguistic similarities, variation in the dependent variable cannot be attributed to these factors. Charrad utilizes the MSSD research design to explain why family codes are more conservative in Morocco and Algeria than in Tunisia. She finds that the level of solidarity among tribal groupings and state strength will be the main determinants (Ibid., 401).[133] Weaker states with stronger

---

[133] The digital [Kindle] version is referenced. Page numbers will vary from the printed editions.

tribes will have more conservative family codes, while stronger states with weaker tribes will have more liberal family codes (Ibid.).

My case selection, much akin to Charrad's, is also contingent on variation between three similar countries. Both Algeria and Morocco have fairly large LGBTQ+ rights movements (though the latter is marginally larger), whereas a queer rights movement did not emerge in Tunisia until after it underwent democratization. The fact that these movements emerged in the more culturally conservative states (Morocco and Algeria), but not in Tunisia, one of the most socially liberal states in the region, is perplexing. These dissimilarities (in otherwise comparable states) make it evident that the MSSD methodology is the most pragmatic research design considering the nature of these three cases.

It was logical to expect a more sizable community of queer rights activists in pre-revolutionary Tunisia for the fact that it has been historically less socially conservative than its Moroccan and Algerian neighbors—both of which had substantial LGBTQ+ rights movements by the late '00s—but that was not the case. Did Tunisia's regime change facilitate the emergence of this movement? If this is the case LGBTQ+ activism should not have emerged in Morocco or Algeria. Therefore, one of two remaining factors must explain this variation: (i) gradual political liberalization in Morocco and Algeria, but not in Tunisia, and (ii) varying degrees of internet access and internet freedom between all three states. What must be understood is (a) why LGBTQ+ movements did not emerge in Tunisia until after it democratized, and (b) why the strength of Morocco's LGBTQ+ movement is stronger than Algeria's. An explanation for these differences will yield an answer to my primary research question: what is the catalyst for LGBTQ+ equality movements in culturally conservative and politically repressive authoritarian regimes?

Variation in Movement Strength is *Not* Due to Political Liberalization

The dependent variable—existence/strength of LGBTQ+ movements—is conspicuous in that it varies across these three cases. One may initially posit that democratization alone may sufficiently catalyze a movement, but if democratization is a factor, this does not explain why Morocco and Algeria have such sizable LGBTQ+ movements even though their regimes have not changed (see Figures 6.1, 6.2). One variable in particular stands out and likely accounts for a significant proportion of variation in the dependent variable: level of access to the internet. Still, an underlying level of political freedom is required for any activism to exist at all. Therefore it will be beneficial to disentangle political liberalization from internet access to see which was more important to the emergence of the Moroccan and Algerian LGBTQ+ movements.

Political liberalization is the expansion of political participation. This entails loosening of prohibitions that bar particular types of political parties from running for office, allowing public protests, and more inclusionary policies with respect to political participation. When it comes to political liberalization states may only be inclined to expand political participation minimally, but democratization involves a total transfer of centralized power from a dictator, military, or political party to the populace (see Schumpeter 1950). The expansion of political participation is extended to everyone in democracies along with protections for civil rights and civil liberties (see Dahl 1971; Ibid., 1989; Schedler 2002).

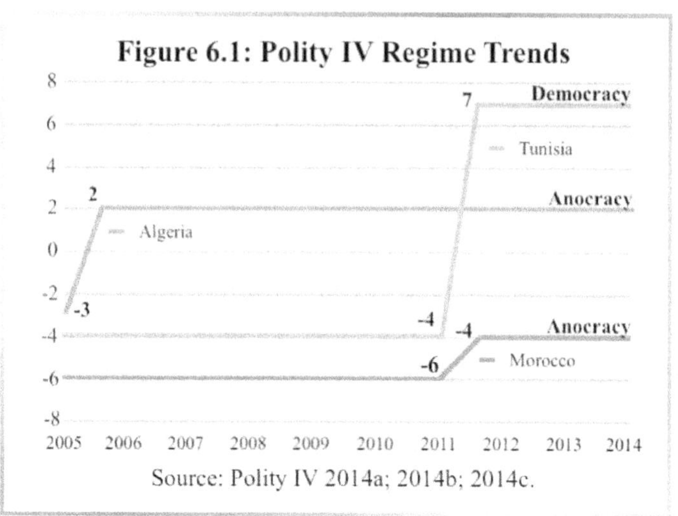

Political Liberalization in Morocco

States have an incentive to liberalize in order to cultivate domestic (as well as international) legitimacy and to extend regime longevity. Joffé (2014) explains that political liberalization has been a gradual process in Morocco that has occurred since the '80s. In the early 2000s substantial social progress was made. Laws surrounding women's rights became more equitable due to updates to the Moroccan family code, and the King also championed policies to ameliorate poverty (Ibid.). Political participation has also expanded. Legislative elections occur in Morocco, but the executive branch is held by the King and remains uncontested. The Party of Justice and Development, which is a moderate Islamic opposition party, maintained control over Morocco's bicameral legislature until the liberal National Rally of Independents won a plurality of votes in 2021, but observers contend Moroccan political parties are merely pseudo-opposition and pose no real threat to the King's monopoly on power (Mekhennet and Baume 2011). A diverse array of political parties are allowed to run, though the monarchy has been successful at co-opting most political opponents (Joffé 2014), so the prospect of substantive political reform or a change in the power structure is unlikely.

When it comes to the materialization of queer rights movements, is it possible that their existence can be attributed to gradual political liberalization? The year when queer rights activism became prominent in Morocco was approximately 2005,[134] but according to Polity IV (2014b, Figure 6.1) the Moroccan regime was consistently autocratic with a score of -6 until 2011, when Polity IV upgraded them to -4. Prior to this change in ranking, Polity IV gave them a 1-point increase in 1999 from -7 to -6 (Ibid.). Between 2004 and 2005 Freedom House (2014) upgraded Morocco's freedom score from 5 to 4.5. However, this slight increase in freedom did not open a window for LGBTQ+ activism to emerge, as Freedom House (2005) attributes this increase to the reformation of Morocco's family codes in 2004, which granted women extensive rights. The reformation of Moroccan family law did not directly benefit

---

[134] This is the year in which Morocco's first gay rights organization was founded.

members of the LGBTQ+ community[135] or increase their net level of freedom. Morocco has not received a higher score from Freedom House since 2005, and Polity IV's 2011 regime upgrade occurred after its LGBTQ+ movement was well underway. Therefore it can be concluded that political liberalization was not a factor that catalyzed its LGBTQ+ movement since any significant political changes that took place did not specifically open the doors for queer activism. Furthermore, the time periods wherein significant political changes occurred were far removed from the time in which LGBTQ+ activism emerged.

Political Liberalization in Algeria

Much like Morocco, Algeria has also liberalized gradually. Though multi-party elections now occur, Algeria is largely a single-party dominant regime. The National Liberation Front (FLN) has a long held monopoly on political power that it has yet to relinquish. Unlike Morocco's executive branch, Algerian presidents must compete in presidential elections, but Freedom House (2013) indicates that these contests are fraudulent and that opposing candidates frequently withdraw from races in protest due to corrupt results. After Algeria's former president, the late Abdelaziz Bouteflika, stepped down after two-decades of power following mass protests, he was succeeded by his Prime Minister (and fellow career politician), Abdelmadjid Tebboune. His ascension was met with widespread skepticism since he was viewed as an entrenched establishment politician who had long

---

[135] Of course, lesbian and bisexual cis women benefited due to increased levels of gender equality, but it did not further their ability to practice homosexuality, nor did it help the LGBTQ+ cause in any way.

been part of Algeria's old guard and was expected to maintain the status quo. This has proven to be true despite Tebboune's attempts to cultivate legitimacy by dissolving parliament in 2021 (ahead of

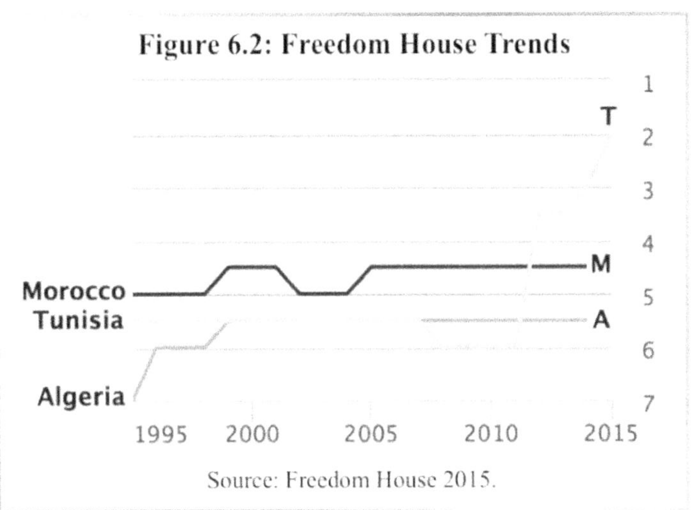

Figure 6.2: Freedom House Trends

Source: Freedom House 2015.

Algeria's scheduled 2022 election) to allow voters to elect new legislators (Harb 2021). It was a thinly veiled attempt to placate disaffected Algerians, but they saw through it. Less than a quarter of eligible voters participated in the election because they did not expect it to facilitate the revolutionary political reforms they were demanding seeing that Alergia represents a type of "electoral authoritarianism that borrows democratic practices without implementing democratic rule" (Ibid.). The popular saying, *'change on the outside, continuity on the inside'* aptly characterizes Algeria's ongoing political climate. Nonetheless, multi-party elections in authoritarian regimes—even if they are little more than window dressing—is still regarded as incremental liberalization since it opens the door to opponents of the regime (even though resistance is futile) and grants them minimal institutional power.

In spite of increased liberalization, primarily in the form of allowing opposition candidates to run for president, Algeria's Freedom House ranking has consistently remained at 5.5 since 1999 (see Figure 6.2). Between 2005 and 2006 Polity IV upgraded Algeria's regime from -3 to 2, which is a 5-point difference (see Figure 6.1). However, this did not open a window for LGBTQ+ activism to emerge. Polity IV (2010) attributes the upgrade to increased transparency during the 2004 presidential election. Moreover, LGBTQ+ activism did not become prevalent until approximately 2009, which is after internet penetration finally surpassed 10% (Internet World Stats 2012b, see Figure 6.4). Therefore it does not appear as though liberalization has caused an Algerian queer rights movement to emerge, nor has it ameliorated social biases against the LGBTQ+ community. The years within which Polity IV and Freedom House upgraded Algeria's regime/ freedom scores are far removed from the time its LGBTQ+ movement materialized.[136] The most recent scoring change by Polity IV (in 2006, see Figure 6.1) was due to greater election transparency, so there is no reason to believe this would directly impact the emergence of a queer rights movement.

Democratization in Tunisia

Tunisia was consistently authoritarian by both Polity IV and Freedom House standards until the revolution (see Figures 6.1 and 6.2 for reference). They did not receive their first score

---

[136] Which is in approximately the late '00s, when its first gay rights organization emerged.

upgrade until 2011; from 6 to 3.5 by Freedom House (2015) and from -4 to 7 by Polity IV (2014a). Prior to democratization Tunisians were prohibited from engaging in political activism. Lutterback describes Ben Ali's regime as "a police state par excellence," which made it difficult for movements of all types to become politically active (2013, 1). Significant political liberalization was the result of democratization in Tunisia. Once Tunisia democratized (and subsequently liberalized politically) a variety of movements came about including a Salafist movement, which was legally barred from existing under the previous regime (Blackshaw 2012). Seeing that the timing of the Tunisian LGBTQ+ movement's emergence coincided with democratization, it would seem reasonable to attribute the emergence of LGBTQ+ activism to the regime change. This assertion is incorrect, however, as it omits nuanced details.

The democratization argument, though logical, has two main problems. First, the social climate for gay and transgender people did not improve upon democratization. While political activists of all stripes—from communists to Salafists—made their political agendas public due to a society-wide inclination to embrace pluralism (seeing as how social solidarity made the revolution possible in the first place), the LGBTQ+ community was perhaps the *single* group whose views remained marginalized after the revolution (Ibid.).

Second, while other new movements such as the Salafist Ansar al-Sharia group, for example, also emerged at approximately the same time as the Tunisian LGBTQ+ movement, Ansar al-Sharia has participated in multiple public demonstrations with upwards of 100 people (see Al Jazeera 2013; Al Arabiya News 2014), whereas queer rights groups in Tunisia such as LGBTI Tunisien or Kelmty were only able to participate in online forms of activism or discreet public events. Even though Tunisia liberalized quite considerably following its 2011 revolution, Tunisian queer rights activists such as Ben Issa and Khaled Azouzi have argued that the social climate was still too hostile for LGBTQ+ people to be public about their political agenda (Blackshaw 2012), hence the need for the internet as a proxy. Simply put, society's embrace of pluralism did not extend to queer causes. Furthermore, if greater pluralism and political liberalization is not what catalyzed queer rights movements in Morocco and Algeria there is no reason to believe it could do so in Tunisia.

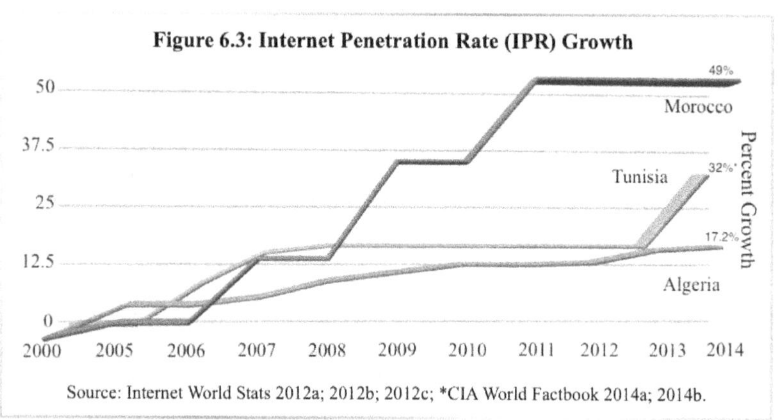

Source: Internet World Stats 2012a; 2012b; 2012c; *CIA World Factbook 2014a; 2014b.

Political liberalization and democratization are useful for the materialization of social movements only insofar as there is at least a minimal level of social acceptability for the cause. This is not the case for gay and trans people, which is why *the internet*— as opposed to the abolition of institutional restrictions on activism via liberalization or democratization—explains the existence of LGBTQ+ activism in Tunisia. If one could attribute the emergence of Tunisia's queer rights movement to liberalization and democratization, it would have been logical to expect them to be on par with other new movements (in terms of strength) that materialized around the same time, but that was not the case. The expansion of political participation in Tunisia may have fostered the emergence of religious, secular, and other ideologically divisive groups, but that did *not* include queer rights groups. Regardless, Tunisian activists were still able to organize public rendezvous and inconspicuous events at the start of their movement thanks to the internet. Any and all queer rights activism was relegated to the online sphere due to the unwelcoming nature of Tunisia's social climate, and that has only begun to change within the last several years; ergo, democratization and political liberalization did not appear to be a casual factor in the materialization of their LGBTQ+ movement. What *does* facilitate the emergence of queer rights movements is the internet and citizens' ability to use it for political purposes.

The Internet's Key Role in the Variation of LGBTQ+ Movement Strength

Variation I: Why Did Activism Not Exist in Tunisia Until After Democratization?

Looking solely at internet penetration rates (IPR) in Morocco, Algeria, and Tunisia in the 2010s it was evident all states were relatively comparable at first glance. Data from CIA World Factbook (2014a; 2014b) indicates Morocco had the highest IPR at 40.1% in 2014. Tunisia came in second with an IPR of 32%, and Algeria's was a modest 12.1% (see Table 2.4), Data from Internet World Stats—though a bit older—indicates slightly higher IPRs for each country; 49% in Morocco (2012a), 17.2% in

Algeria (2012b), and 32% in Tunisia (2012c) [see Figure 6.3]. Raw percentages are somewhat misleading when it comes to why LGBTQ+ activism did not emerge in Tunisia. A more substantive examination of the level of freedom citizens have to use the internet is also required.

In the event 100% of the population had access to the internet it would not serve as a viable political utility unless citizens were able to use it *freely*—that is—there is only minimal amounts of governmental interference or restrictions on websites (especially ones used for mobilization purposes such as Facebook, X [known as Twitter at the time], and YouTube or their regional equivalents), or citizens have the ability to easily bypass such restrictions. An in-depth examination reveals precisely why a Tunisian LGBTQ+ movement never took off under Ben Ali; because the Tunisian government was successful at suppressing citizens' freedom on the internet. This has not been the case in Morocco and Algeria.

Freedom House (2014) ranked Tunisia's overall internet freedom as "not free" in 2011—their last year as an authoritarian regime. Using a 100-point scale, Freedom House scored Tunisia's overall internet freedom 81 out of 100 in 2011 (with 1 denoting total freedom and 100 signaling a complete lack thereof) and explains how there were limitations on content, censorship of political bloggers, and punishment for internet users that sought to engage in online political activism (Freedom House 2011). It was not uncommon for the Tunisian government to stringently censor content on the internet and restrict access to websites of the regime's choice.

There was a four-year window when the internet could have been relatively useful as a political tool in Tunisia; particularly between the time infrastructure for broadband was being built[137] in 2005 up until 2009, which is when the government began to crackdown on the dissemination of user-created content once internet penetration increased (Ibid.). Internet access was likely not sufficient to catalyze a queer rights movement by 2005, and once more citizens finally gained access to the internet their ability to freely use it was restricted. Ben Ali likely saw the internet as a threat to his regime. As internet penetration increased, so too did censorship. Incremental losses in internet freedom was correlated with growth in penetration rates according to Freedom House (2011). There were restrictions on websites critical for political mobilization such as YouTube and Facebook. That was not the case with Morocco and Algeria. What has changed since 2011 in Tunisia is its level of internet freedom. As of 2012 Freedom House (2014) upgraded Tunisia's internet freedom ranking to "partly free" once much of the restrictions were abolished and censorship dissipated after Ben Ali fled the country.

Though Freedom House does not report levels of internet freedom in Algeria (and did not report on internet freedom in Morocco until 2013 [see Freedom House 2014]), there is still evidence to suggest citizens in both states enjoyed a much higher degree of internet freedom. According to OpenNet Initiative (2009a) the Algerian government maintains control over the internet infrastructure, and as a result, it will occasionally utilize it as a security apparatus for surveillance purposes, but the Algerian government does not filter political and/or social content, nor did it do so once internet penetration increased. There are exceptions

---

[137] Broadband is important namely because faster speeds will allow for uploads/downloads of larger files, such as images and videos, which could prove useful for political purposes in order to document government abuse and share political messages.

to this, as the regime attempted to stymie citizens' access to Facebook during the 2011 Arab spring (Ramdani 2011), but this was due to extraordinary circumstances and is not the norm.

There was little evidence that the Moroccan government heavily censored content on the internet (OpenNet Initiative 2009b) at least until recently. There were particular instances when they selectively filtered some content (such as social media and photo board sites), but this was also rare and typically out of the norm (OpenNet Initiative 2009b). For all intents and purposes, the LGBTQ+ community in these two states could organize freely online. The consequences of this are evident, as queer Moroccans and Algerians capitalized on internet freedom (as well as increased access to the internet) to launch their movements.

The idea for Kif-Kif, Morocco's first formal queer rights organization, manifested on an online forum for LGBTQ+ people (Association Alouen 2011). As the number of users grew, members sought to become active in politics by formulating an actual organization to represent their interests. Kif-Kif is now considered the leading queer rights association in the Maghreb by its sister movement in Algeria (Ibid.). Kif-Kif's Facebook page has more than 362,000 likes and 391,000 followers. LGBTQ+ activism in Morocco has been deeply entrenched with the internet historically. A majority of LGBTQ-tailored resources—ranging from magazines to online campaigns—are coordinated and staged exclusively online. The internet is fundamental to LGBTQ+ activism in authoritarian regimes, and because queer Tunisians were unable to fully take advantage of the access they had to the internet, they were unable to engage in activism or forge a viable movement.

Variation II: Why is Morocco's LGBTQ+ Movement Slightly Larger Than Algeria's Despite Equivalent Levels of Internet Freedom in Both Countries?

Morocco's LGBTQ+ movement is slightly more advanced and active than Algeria's, but this can be explained simply by the fact that Morocco has a higher percentage of internet users than Algeria, and additionally, its IPR accelerated more speedily than Algeria's. By the end of 2000 Algeria only had 50,000 internet users whereas Morocco had double that amount irrespective of the fact that Algeria has roughly six million more citizens than Morocco (Internet World Stats 2014). By 2014 Algeria had about 6.7 million internet users, but in contrast, Morocco had four times that amount (Ibid.). The exponential expansion of internet access in Morocco in comparison to Algeria makes two things evident: (i) the Algerian LGBTQ+ movement emerged several years after Morocco's for the fact that Algeria was slower at increasing citizens' access to the internet, and (ii) Morocco's LGBTQ+ movement is slightly more advanced/active than Algeria's because much more people have access to the internet in Morocco than in Algeria. Furthermore, around the time LGBTQ+ activism became more prominent in Algeria internet-related factors had recently changed; specifically, internet access became more widely available.

Belson (2014) demonstrates that Algeria's expansion of broadband infrastructure was substantial in 2013; it increased by 1,000% (2). This meant the activist-minded LGBTQ+ people with internet access were no longer relegated to 56k dial-up, which made political mobilization less challenging. Social media sites such as X (formerly Twitter), Facebook, and YouTube became easily accessible to those with broadband connections. However, broadband users accounted for a very small portion of total internet users in the region in the 2010s; approximately 1-3% in Morocco, 2-4% in Algeria, and 3-5% in Tunisia (GSMA 2014, 19). About one in five broadband users in Morocco and Tunisia were smartphone users, whereas just one in twenty Algerians accessed broadband internet through smartphones (Ibid.).

The Middle East and Africa has, since 2011, had the second-largest user base of mobile phone users in the world behind Asia (eMarketer 2013). In 2011 they had 445.6 million users, by 2013 they had reached 525.8 million (Ibid.). Mobile phone speeds of 3G and 4G[138] saw a steady increase of penetration in the region overall during the 2010s, but in comparison with Morocco and Tunisia—whose total 3G/4G smartphone users accounted for approximately 20% of their total broadband base—the proportion of Algeria's 3G and 4G mobile phone users made up less than 5% out of its entire base of broadband users (GSMA 2014, 19). Much like their internet infrastructure, Morocco was ahead of Algeria and Tunisia when it came to 3G speeds in the 2010s. Morocco rolled out its 3G network in 2007, which explains why the proportion of fixed to non-fixed broadband users (that is, those with access through a computer versus a mobile device) was higher in Morocco, although Tunisia was quick to follow due to its small population and geographical size (Ibid., 21). Algeria was also slightly behind Morocco and Tunisia when it came to cellphone adoption in the 2010s; 16% of Moroccans and 17% of Tunisians owned cellular telephones in contrast with only 13% of Algerians (22).

---

[138] Speeds above 3G technically qualifies as broadband while 4G is a step up from that. Other options, which are particularly slower, are 2G and lower. The latter speeds were still more common (see GSMA 2014).

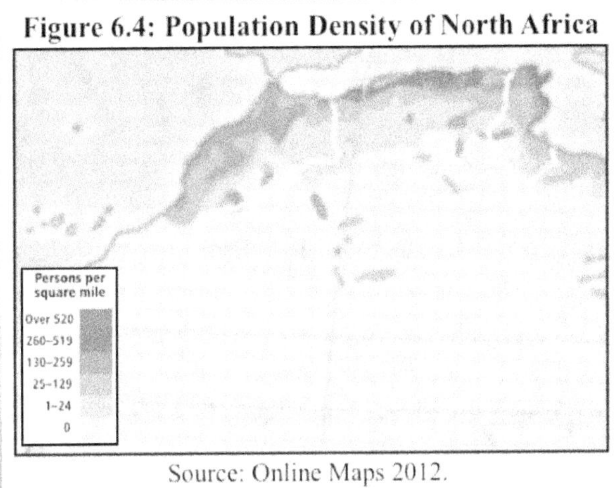

Figure 6.4: Population Density of North Africa

Source: Online Maps 2012.

Upon an examination of these statistics it becomes clear that the reason Morocco's LGBTQ+ movement is slightly stronger than Algeria's is because access to the internet was much higher in Morocco at the onset of these movements. This is not necessarily surprising when accounting for three factors: (i) Algeria's population is larger, thus making it difficult to reach more citizens, (ii) geographically, it is larger, which complicates the building of infrastructure, and (iii) its population density is fairly consolidated (with an urbanization rate of over 70% [CIA World Factbook 2014d]), but there are large pockets of rural populations dispersed throughout the state (see Figure 6.4). These factors made the implementation of broadband more difficult. Algeria had a lot more ground to cover than its neighbors; specifically, 2,381,741 square kilometers (Ibid.). Even when infrastructure is built factors such as reliability, speed consistency, and whether websites and internet hosts have enough bandwidth to handle heavy traffic impacts activists' ability to organize. Therefore, Algerian queers' ability to catch up with its Moroccan peers hinged on how fast its government could increase overall internet availability (and, of course, maintain a sustained level of internet freedom).

Summary of Primary Findings

When it comes to the role of the internet, it is clear that the Tunisian LGBTQ+ community was unable to emerge before democratization for the fact that they lacked adequate freedom to use the internet for political mobilization. Hopkins (2012) explains how Tunisia has long been been known as an "enemy of the internet." Once Tunisia democratized, this trend ceased as of 2012, which is the same year LGBTQ+ activism began to materialize on Facebook and become visible to international observers. What is perceptible is the speed in which LGBTQ+ movements strengthen once they develop. The Algerian LGBTQ+ movement was barely discernible in 2008, but that changed by 2009. Until 2014 the Tunisian LGBTQ+ movement was very small, but they became a moderately organized political faction fairly quickly. Tunisia's movement swiftly advanced to Tier 2 by 2015 and predictably became a full-fledged Tier 3 movement by around 2018. The strength and growth of these movements will likely continue to accelerate upon greater availability of the internet, granted current levels of freedom on the web remain consistent.

These findings indicate that internet freedom is more important than penetration rates for the creation of LGBTQ+ movements seeing that even though only a small portion of Algeria's total population had access to the internet in the late 2000s, a queer rights movement still managed to emerge. However, the overall strength of LGBTQ+ movements will be determined by growth of internet penetration rates. Internet freedom allows queer rights movements to exist, whereas IPR rates will determine the strength and size of these movements once they materialize.

In terms of internet freedom, all three cases examined in this chapter were on par during the rise of LGBTQ+ activism in Tunisia. According to Alexa (2015a) websites utilized most frequently for purposes of political mobilization (such as social media and video-sharing sites) were incredibly popular in the 2010s. Facebook was the second most popular website in Morocco followed by YouTube, while X (formerly Twitter) was the 21st most popular website. In Algeria and Tunisia, Facebook was the most popular website and YouTube was third most popular (Ibid., 2015b; Similar Web 2014). Even web content that is thought to contribute to social immorality such as pornographic websites were among the most visited websites in these states (Ibid.). This indicates that Morocco, Algeria, and Tunisia all allowed for an adequate level of internet freedom by the mid-2010s.

Conclusion

It is clear that variation in the strength of movements is contingent on differences between levels of freedom on the internet as well as overall access to it. In Morocco and Algeria LGBTQ+ individuals were able to use the internet freely to mobilize, but in contrast, the Tunisian government heavily blocked content and prohibited websites that could have potentially been used for purposes of political mobilization. Once Tunisia democratized and restrictions on internet freedom became more lax, queer activism emerged almost immediately. This is a

Figure 6.5: Illustration of Movement Strength Crossed by Internet Trends

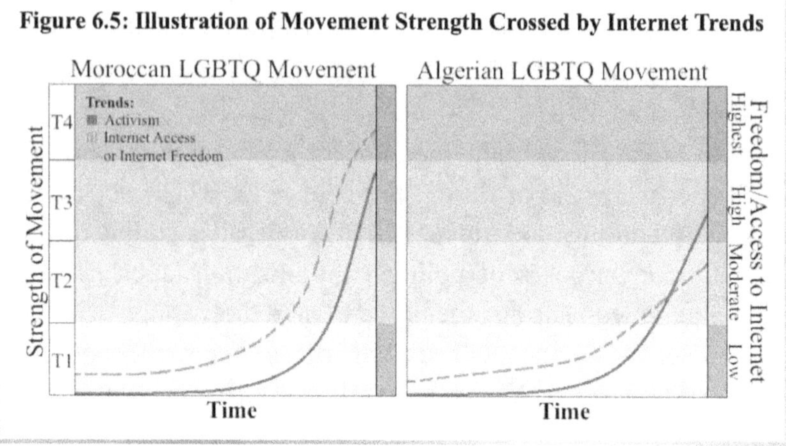

very important finding that has significant implications on sociological and political science research for social movements.

The strength of movements is clearly correlated with the level of access activists have to the internet (see examples in Figure 6.5, modeled after Tammen [2000], 22-23: Figures 1.9 and 1.10). This finding unequivocally validates the internet mobilization hypothesis. The internet was the sole factor that varied across all of these cases, and once internet conditions changed, so too did the dependent variable.

With respect to the social blowback and political liberalization hypotheses, there is a lack of evidence to support both of them. Repression and activism are correlated, but there is no evidence a causal relationship exists. Although there are often intense episodes of persecution waged against LGBTQ+ communities in these states—especially in Morocco—the overall level of repression against the LGBTQ+ community has remained consistent, so it seems unlikely that episodes of persecution would alone catalyze activism. Episodes of persecution would undoubtedly quantify existing motivations to initiate a queer rights movement, but there is insufficient evidence to suggest it sufficed as a catalyst for LGBTQ+ activism in Morocco, Algeria, or Tunisia.

When it comes to the political liberalization hypothesis, it does not yield much explanatory value in the three aforementioned cases. Political liberalization in Morocco and Algeria did not open new doors for LGBTQ+ activists, nor did it occur in a time frame that coincides with the emergence of their queer rights movements. Increased liberalization due to democratization in Tunisia also does not explain the emergence of the Tunisian LGBTQ+ movement. Though it is true that queer activism emerged after Tunisia democratized and consequentially liberalized, Morocco and Algeria did not democratize and still witnessed the materialization of LGBTQ+ rights movements. Also, other movements have flourished since democratization in Tunisia and frequently participate in public protests, but LGBTQ+ activists—to this day—are still *very* cautious about public protests (although there are exceptions). The liberalization hypothesis may explain why movements for other types of postmaterialist causes exist in authoritarian regimes, but it does not explain the emergence of queer rights movements in this small-N study and will not likely be applicable to LGBTQ+ movements in other MENA states. Insofar as the three cases in this chapter are concerned, the internet mobilization hypothesis best explains variation in the strength and existence of movements.

This analysis shows that socially unacceptable causes such as gay and transgender equality movements are able to exist—and even thrive—in authoritarian regimes in the MENA due to the arrival of new political resources that give them the ability to covertly mobilize online and engage in activism anonymously.

Government censorship stymied any and all activism from occurring online in Tunisia, but once citizens were granted the ability to use the internet freely, LGBTQ+ activists were able to construct advocacy-oriented pages on social media websites and ultimately formed a robust queer rights movement.

Furthermore, though Morocco and Algeria both have fairly large queer rights movements, Morocco's was (and still is) slightly larger. Alouen, one of Algeria's leading queer rights groups, refers to the Moroccan queer rights organization Kif-Kif as the leading LGBTQ+ organization in the Maghreb (Association Alouen 2011), and for good reason. Morocco's collective LGBTQ+ movement was more sizable and active because the eligibility pool of queer citizens that were able to engage in activism in the 2010s was larger simply due to a higher level of internet access. Conversely, many Algerians did not have access to the internet in spite of adequate internet freedom; however, enough citizens had access for a Tier 3 LGBTQ+ movement to exist by the 2010s. These findings draw us to the following conclusion: internet freedom as well as access to the internet catalyzes LGBTQ+ movements in authoritarian regimes because queer citizens can avoid social persecution and directly engage in anonymous activism due to their ability to clandestinely organize.

Now that a comprehensive evaluation has been done the main research question of this book can confidently be answered; what causes queer rights movements to emerge in authoritarian regimes in the MENA? *They emerge when new political opportunities materialize—in this case it was the internet.* The internet gave LGBTQ+ activists in Morocco, Algeria, and Tunisia a safe conduit to engage in activism. For this reason, it is now known that LGBTQ+ movements require the internet and internet freedom to exist in conservative, politically repressive states.

The State of LGBTQ+ Activism in 2024 Following Changes to Internet Freedom

By the late 2010s Tunisia's LGBTQ+ movement surpassed Morocco's in size and strength and, as of the early 2020s, Tier 4 is arguably within reach. The ongoing strength of Tunisia's LGBTQ+ movement in spite of a decline in democracy is further evidence that political liberalization is not needed for queer movements to exist. What *is* needed is sustained internet freedom and increased internet access for movement growth. While President Saïed has cracked down on internet freedom in 2021 and 2022 with censorious new decrees curtailing online political speech, the internet is still much freer today than it was in pre-revolutionary Tunisia under Ben Ali. Though Freedom House (2022a) only considers the internet in Tunisia to be "partly free"—with a score of 61 out of 100—it still enjoys the "highest" level of internet freedom in the Arab world. Furthermore, internet penetration in Tunisia has doubled since the emergence of LGBTQ+ activism with a 66.7% IPR as of 2022 (Kemp 2022, also see CIA World Fact Book 2020). Growth in internet penetration coincides with an increase in the strength and size of Tunisia's LGBTQ+ movement. This further illustrates how (i) internet availability and internet freedom plays an integral role in the *materialization* of LGBTQ+ movements in the MENA (as the internet mobilization hypothesis has demonstrated), while (ii) potential for *growth and survivability* of LGBTQ+ movements in this region hinges on sustained internet freedom following the birth of the movement.

Growth of Morocco's LGBTQ+ movement has slowed, but not stagnated. It is still incrementally expanding into the 2020s, but it has seemingly not yet advanced to Tier 4. A cause for slower growth in Morocco's LGBTQ+ movement could be attributed to new restrictions on internet freedom. Between 2016 and 2022 internet freedom decreased by 5-points based on Freedom House's scoring. An increase in online surveillance as well as instances of retaliation against critics of the monarchy have been reported by Freedom House (2022b), resulting in a score of 51 out of 100 and designation of "partly free" (down from 56 in 2016 and 53 in 2021). While Morocco's new censorship laws do not single out queer people per se, the crackdown may have had a chilling effect on political speech overall and discouraged activism from queer rights groups. Although, in 2023 Freedom House gave Morocco a score of 53 out of 100—a 2-point increase—following improvements to internet coverage and no new restrictions to internet freedom (see Freedom House 2023). It is too early to tell if this is the start of a trend in the direction of enhanced internet freedom again in Morocco, but more restrictions must be lifted for Morocco to be on par with its level of freedom in the 2000s and 2010s. Despite new restrictions on internet freedom, Morocco's LGBTQ+ movement has gradually grown nevertheless due to an expansion of internet availability. Morocco's internet penetration rate expanded to 88.1% in 2023 (Galal 2023a), a 39-point increase since 2014. As internet penetration in Morocco reaches most of the population, the law of diminishing returns suggests IPR may no longer be a useful indicator of LGBTQ+ movement growth and strength. Since the overwhelming majority of Morocco's population now has access to the internet it is logical to assume future growth of LGBTQ+ activism will hinge almost exclusively on internet freedom going forward.

As for Algeria, the overall situation is still bleak. Homosexuality is still illegal and not tolerated by society, government and Algeria's judicial system. Organizations promoting LGBTQ+ rights are not allowed to exist, and furthermore, an attempt to register organizations inconsistent with Algeria's "public morals" could endanger the lives of individuals seeking official recognition (see Human Rights Watch 2020). Nonetheless, LGBTQ+ activism is still alive and well in Algeria to the chagrin of the government thanks to the internet. Galal (2023b) reports steady growth in internet availability with an IPR of 63%, with mobile internet subscriptions drastically increasing. Algeria's significant expansion of internet availability coincides with more restrictions imposed by the government. The now defunct Free Internet Project[139] last placed Algeria under the broad category of "internet censorship or lack of internet freedoms" for free speech violations and overall refusal to protect privacy that is supposed to be constitutionally mandated (see The Free Internet Project in references). Internet surveillance is commonplace under the pretense of "national security" and the government has arrested citizens for political posts on Facebook (Freedom House 2023b). On the subject of social media, the U.S. Department of State (2022) reports numerous instances of outright bans—albeit temporarily—on sites like Facebook and X (formerly Twitter). Moreover, internet service providers "face criminal penalties for the material and websites they host" (Ibid.); meaning there's no law equivalent to Section 230 in the United States, therefore both the user *and* the web host could be prosecuted for uploading a video deemed illegal (assuming they are unwilling to comply with government demands to remove said content). Despite limited internet freedom, LGBTQ+ activism in Algeria continues to

---

[139] The Free Internet Project announced on December 17th, 2023 they were ending their project (see Free Internet Project in references).

persist since users can still protect their anonymity, which is possible for the fact that the Algerian government has yet to ban the use of VPNs, meaning internet restrictions can be circumvented fairly easily, although Algerians are still wise to exercise caution.

Other Arguments

There are three other potential arguments that counter the internet mobilization hypothesis. The first posits that the internet is not the de facto method of mobilization for LGBTQ+ activists in the MENA region since public pro-gay rights demonstrations have taken place in Lebanon; therefore, queer rights activism must not be contingent on the internet. Instead, the internet merely simplifies the process by making mobilization and collective action more streamlined. Second, one cannot identify a 'tipping point' wherein internet access/freedom became prominent enough to allow for the emergence of a queer rights movement. Third, as M. Roberts' (1995) hypothesis posits, the LGBTQ+ communities —mostly gay and bisexual men—are disproportionately impacted by HIV/AIDS in comparison to heterosexuals, which could spawn gay organizing efforts (Mumtaz et al. 2011). Though HIV/AIDS rates in the MENA are comparatively lower, it is still worthwhile to examine this as a potential catalyst for gay rights activism in the region.

Argument I: The Role of Internet in Queer Rights Protests

The first counterargument contends that the internet is not essential to LGBTQ+ activism in the MENA region, otherwise public demonstrations by queer rights advocates in Lebanon would not have occurred. Instead, the internet is most commonly used by LGBTQ+ activists only because it makes political mobilization and coordination easier. The latter component of this counter argument is accurate. The internet *has* opened the doors for all types of activism. Even existing feminist movements have adopted online campaign strategies to pressure governments. For instance, prior to Saudi Arabia's reversal of its ban on female drivers in 2018, Saudi feminists used to initiate annual calls to defy the female driving ban by devising coordinated hashtag campaigns on X (formerly Twitter), and by uploading videos of themselves driving to YouTube (Naar 2013). There is no reason to doubt the utility of the internet as a tool for *all* activists; however, this counter argument falls apart quickly upon further inspection.

The case of public demonstrations by LGBTQ+ activists in Lebanon is wholly isolated. Although Moroccan LGBTQ+ activists, for example, have transcended their online roots, any and all demonstrations or marches occur abroad. Even its chief LGBTQ+ organization, Kif-Kif, is not headquartered in Morocco, but instead resides in Spain. The Algerian LGBTQ+ Facebook group, Union des Gays et Lesbiennes en Algérie, was able to successfully mobilize a domestic public protest only to the extent that candles were used as stand-ins for the activists themselves (Afrol News 2010). Public demonstrations—while not unheard of —are highly unlikely given the social climate in these states. Nevertheless, if one had to select a state whereby the likelihood for a public demonstration is greater, Lebanon would be it.

Lebanon, much akin to Israel and Türkiye, is unique in that homosexuality is comparatively less controversial there. Pew Research Center (2013) indicates that Lebanon is one of the least hostile countries in the region towards the notion of homosexuality; 18% of respondents believe "society should accept homosexuality." This is in contrast with many other states such as Egypt, Jordan, and Tunisia where four percent or less believe homosexuality should be accepted (Ibid.). This reveals that nearly one in five Lebanese individuals are accepting of LGBTQ+ people, thus signaling that public demonstrations—though not the preeminent method—will not be entirely out of the question. Given the large amount of Lebanese citizens that accept homosexuality, this also indicates a substantial proportion of that support comes from heterosexuals, which implies the social climate is more hospitable to gay people in Lebanon. Moreover, according to Freedom House (2015) Lebanon is one of few states in the region considered to be "partly free" with an overall score of 4.5. This further illustrates that its political climate is distinct in comparison with its neighbors.

Even if the conditions in Lebanon were less conducive to the possibility of public LGBTQ+ rights demonstrations occurring, the internet mobilization hypothesis—like all hypotheses—is probabilistic and can account for a small margin of error. However, Lebanese LGBTQ+ activism would also not exist without the internet, as Helem—the region's first formal gay rights organization and coordinator of Lebanese public protest events—exists solely *because* of it (see Helem 2014). Torbey (2005) writes, "George Azzi, the group's co-ordinator [sic], says the idea first came to life in an internet chat room whose members decided to organise an association." This trend is consistent with many other formal queer rights organizations across the region.

The internet is still the main conduit for queer rights activism in Lebanon. Informal online-based organizations like the Lebanese LGBT Media Monitor mobilized effective online campaigns through X (formerly Twitter) such as the #HammamRaid and #NoMoreRaids in an effort to raise awareness of instances of legal persecution against individuals in attendance of LGBTQ-friendly clubs (Littauer 2014). Still, the internet mobilization hypothesis does not contend that LGBTQ+ activism cannot ever transcend its online roots—because that is certainly a possibility—but the initial formulation of queer rights movements in authoritarian regimes is contingent on access to the internet and web freedom. The success of the movement will dictate how long it will be limited to the web.

Argument II: Lack of Accuracy

The second argument confronts the fact that it is fairly difficult to pinpoint an exact percentage in which internet penetration becomes sufficient for the emergence of LGBTQ+ activism. Such an argument is premised on the false assumption that activism will emerge immediately following increased access to the internet. Even in the event it were the case that a tipping point—a percentage in which internet penetration becomes sufficient to catalyze queer rights movements—could be identified, there would be a great deal of planning and coordination on behalf of activists, which would take time, thus implying the emergence would be delayed by a couple of years. However, once internet penetration becomes sufficient, by the time a queer rights movement emerges and is visible, the IPR would likely change. Another reason it is difficult to identify a precise tipping point is because MENA internet stats are not released annually. For these reasons, pinpointing a precise IPR percentage is onerous.

With the case of Kelmty, an informal gay rights organization in Tunisia, it did not emerge immediately following the revolution. Ben Ali was ousted in early 2011, but the Kelmty

Facebook page was not created until 2012. In 2014 it attained 1,500 likes, and by 2015 it finally reached over 2,500 likes and established an official website that directs traffic to its bevy of social media links. It was only classified as an informal organization by the mid-2010s. This is a seemingly appropriate time frame—two to three years—to discern whether newly created Facebook groups will morph into informal organizations. LGBTQ+ activism in Algeria had a slow start, but received a boost due to a number of changes in factors related to internet access (increased internet penetration, expansion of broadband, and growth of mobile phone use).

Lastly, specification of an exact percentage of internet access that is required to catalyze LGBTQ+ movements is unnecessary. Its absence does not detract from the overall validity of the internet mobilization hypothesis. Ascertaining truth about the cause-effect relationship between the internet and LGBTQ+ activism is what matters most. In the event change in either (a) the existence of queer rights movements, or (b) an increase/decrease in a movement's strength occurs, one can verify that the internet is the cause by observing whether factors such as internet access or internet freedom has also changed.

Argument III: HIV/AIDS as an Alternate Explanation

Finally, M. Roberts (1995) states that regimes in developing countries fail to target HIV prevention programs towards its LGBTQ+ communities (248), thus creating an inadvertent gap in knowledge of safe-sex practices within the community. A lack of safe-sex knowledge almost always overwhelmingly impacts younger demographics. Omission of safe-sex practices in HIV prevention programs for same-sex intercourse is likely dependent on a regime's aversion to or outright denial of the existence of homosexuality. This has been the case in Iran and Russia (see Penketh 2008; Sieczkowski 2014). It may also be because providing such information to queer communities could potentially be seen as a tacit endorsement or legitimization of homosexuality, which may not be culturally permissible. Failure to provide safe-sex education to LGBTQ+ communities will lead to a greater concentration of those infected within that community (M. Roberts 1995, 248).

This is a reasonable operating hypothesis, however, it is incredibly difficult to control for sexual orientation when attempting to gauge the prevalence of HIV/AIDS in these states. Infection rates among adults between the ages of 15 and 49-years-old are relatively low in Algeria, Morocco, and Tunisia. Approximately only .10% of citizens in these states are infected (CIA World Factbook 2014c; Sufian 2004). Evidence does suggest that of those few that are infected in the region, gay and bisexual men are impacted disproportionately by HIV/AIDS for the fact that male-to-male sexual contact (MSM) increases one's chances of becoming infected, statistically speaking (Mumtaz et al. 2011).

A sample size of 1,778 individuals indicates that the rate of infection among gay and/or bisexual males in Tunisia is exceedingly high at 4.6%—which is nearly one in twenty gay men —although this percentage is lower than the likes of Egypt, Iran, Pakistan, and Sudan (Ibid., 6). A much smaller sample size of 90 gay/bisexual men in Morocco indicates that the rate of infection among them is 4.4% (Ibid.). This is high as well, but the sample size is too small to hold weight. Data on HIV/AIDS prevalence among Algeria's gay community has not been collected.

Due to the lack of gay activism under Ben Ali's repressive regime, it seems improbable that a high prevalence of HIV/AIDS among gay and bisexual men would alone catalyze a queer rights movement. If this were the case, assuming the infection rates have remained high among gay and bisexual men, a movement would have likely emerged sooner in order to combat it from spreading further. That is not to say gay/bisexual men did not desire to combat the spread of HIV/AIDS in their community, but they likely opted not to in order to avoid persecution or being outed. Therefore M. Roberts' hypothesis—if it could be validated— would not necessarily diminish the internet's role in catalyzing gay rights movements no more than the social blowback hypothesis would. As is the case during periods of intense persecution, HIV/AIDS may enhance existing *motivations* to engage in activism, but it would not give activists the *ability* to mobilize.

If it were the case that there was an increased prevalence of HIV/AIDS among gay communities in the MENA, it would be added to a long catalog of reasons why political mobilization of the LGBTQ+ community is all the more necessary, but the *opportunity* to engage in activism (which is most important) will ultimately be dependent on access to the internet, not AID/AIDS. M Roberts' hypothesis, in part, follows the new social movement line of reasoning, but that theory is more appropriate for explaining why LGBTQ+ activism emerges in democratic and/or nominally democratic regimes. Furthermore, M. Roberts' hypothesis is not inclusive of gay and bisexual women or transgender and non-binary people, so it cannot explain why they also participate in LGBTQ+ activism in authoritarian states since he purports that gay men are the only ones impacted by HIV or AIDS. If this were applicable to the MENA, we should expect only gay and bisexual men to fight for queer rights, but that is not the reality. The internet mobilization hypothesis explains why *all* members of the LGBTQ+ community engage in activism in authoritarian regimes.

Overall, there is an insufficient amount of evidence to support M. Roberts' HIV/AIDS hypothesis. That is not to say it is not relevant elsewhere, but it cannot be proven that HIV/AIDS single-handedly catalyzed LGBTQ+ movements in Tunisia or Morocco. If it could, one would have expected to see the materialization of LGBTQ+ activism prior to democratization in Tunisia and liberalization in Morocco. This hypothesis is more suited for democracies or nominally democratic regimes seeing that it rests on the assumption that queer rights movements are *able* to emerge in any social climate, but that is not the case. New political opportunities (i.e. the internet) explains the existence of queer rights movements in authoritarian regimes.

CHAPTER 7

Conclusion & Implications for Social Movement Research

This book supports the claim that new political resources affords actors in authoritarian regimes the opportunity to engage in activism. Greater availability and freedom on the internet explains variation in the strength and existence of LGBTQ+ movements in Morocco, Algeria, and Tunisia. Upon further political liberalization in all three states, queer rights activists were still unable to engage in more orthodox methods of activism (e.g. public demonstrations, lobbying politicians, activism via proxy groups such as human rights organizations, NGOS, unions, or Islamic associations) due to the controversial nature of their causes. The internet was the *one* conduit with which they were able to convey their message. This finding should change the way sociologists and political scientists think about social movements. The *ability* of activists to politically mobilize is a key factor when it comes to why movements emerge.

The prospect of equality for sexual and gender minorities is too contentious in these states for activists to be open about their political ambitions. They lack political allies to fight on their behalf. Civil rights advocacy groups in the region, by and large, have been unwilling to take up LGBTQ+ causes. The Egyptian Organization for Human Rights has publicly distanced themselves from queer rights activists for "religious and cultural reasons" (Masriya 2014). Such a move may not have been influenced by homophobia or transphobia though, as associating themselves with gays, lesbians, bisexuals, and transgender individuals would most certainly detract from their domestic legitimacy, which could impact their funding and put them in direct opposition with governments, thus threatening their existence. As a result, most domestic civil rights groups will avoid adopting queer rights platforms. This leaves members of the LGBTQ+ community to fend for themselves. The internet has provided them cover in Middle Eastern and North African states. It allows them to stake their claim in politics without the fear of retribution from social conservatives, religious fundamentalists, homophobes and transphobes, or the state. A brief examination of other cases indicates the internet plays a fundamental role in LGBTQ+ movements not just in Morocco, Algeria, and Tunisia, but throughout the region as well.

A Brief Overview of Other LGBTQ+ Movements in the MENA

Lack of an in-depth examination of variables such as regime type, political freedom, internet penetration rates, freedom on the net, and smartphone usage will not produce a nuanced understanding of LGBTQ+ movements in the region. However, seeing as how it has been established that the internet plays a key role in queer rights activism in the Middle East and North Africa, a brief overview of the methods employed by other LGBTQ+ activists will still be fruitful in order to demonstrate the overall importance of the internet to their cause.

X (formerly Twitter) is highly valuable to queer rights activists in the MENA. Hashtag campaigns are a popular tactic primarily because they raise a great deal of both domestic and international attention. Egyptian LGBTQ+ activists have initiated the "#SolidaritywithEgyptLGBT" and "#StopJailingGays" hashtag campaigns (Sheils 2014; Feder 2014). In Lebanon the Lebanese LGBT Media Monitor, an online organization, has been instrumental at coordinating effective hashtag campaigns such as the #HammamRaid and #NoMoreRaids in an effort to raise awareness of raids on queer-friendly night clubs (Littauer 2014). These campaigns are mostly initiated by informal organizations that exclusively exist online. These types of advocacy groups have become increasingly common. The aforementioned Lebanese LGBT Media Monitor has attained a significant amount of visibility. Multiple informal online-exclusive organizations have also materialized in Egypt: "Arabs4Tolerance" and "GayEgypt" being two with arguably the most exposure (Masriya 2014).

The LGBTQ+ movement in Iran, akin to all other movements in the MENA region, was also initiated online (see "Iranian Queer Organization" 2015). Queer Iranians have constructed both formal and informal organizations and have also co-opted domestic and international allies, but activism via social media is the tactic they use most frequently. In 2011 gay and lesbian Iranians uploaded videos of themselves sharing their stories of legal and social persecution (Cohen 2011). Moreover, Tehran's gay community uploaded photographs of themselves with rainbow flags and anti-homophobia signs to an Iranian social networking website (Fisher 2012). Informal organizations that maintain a strong presence online have acquired appreciable followings. The Facebook group "Yes People! We Do Exist!" was created in 2012 and has accumulated thousands of likes (see "Yes People! We Do Exist!" 2015). Iran's LGBTQ+ movement also relies exclusively on the internet for domestic activism. This is consistent with other LGBTQ+ groups in the region. Public demonstrations and pride marches are not an option unless they transpire outside of Iranian territory.

Notably, the internet is censored quite heavily in Iran, and as a result, these restrictions may prevent its LGBTQ+ movement from becoming too sizable (Lee 2013). Irrespectively, a queer rights movement was able to materialize for the fact that many citizens, if not most, are able to circumvent governmental firewalls by using a variety of popular software applications that either mask their IP addresses or generate foreign ones by using VPNs (Ibid.). Even though the Iranian government blocks access to popular social networking websites like Facebook (Eremenko 2013), many Iranians are still able to access it according to Lee. For those unable to bypass government censorship, domestic social networking websites such as Joopea are viable alternatives for LGBTQ+ activists. Queer rights activists in other states with heavy restrictions on internet freedom such as Saudi Arabia (Stern 2014) have not been as successful as Iranians at circumventing governmental restrictions on the internet. The Saudi monarchy still censors the internet heavily, and because of this one can speculate that a queer rights movement will not materialize there until that changes (Ibid.). Notwithstanding some exceptions, many other MENA states have seen the manifestation of LGBTQ+ rights movements.

If these movements are becoming more common, why are they still mostly ignored by social scientists? Queer rights activism in authoritarian regimes likely does not get attention for three reasons: (i) their movements are comparatively small in contrast with other regional political groups, thereby making them difficult to measure, (ii) information on them is sparse, and (iii) there is a common misconception that either (a) these movements do not exist, or (b) that Western conceptions of homosexuality are foreign to the region.

Why Social Scientists Should Not Forego the Study of Queer Rights in the MENA

The latter cultural relativist claim is made by Bradley (2010). He critiques "Western-style gays rights activism" in the Middle East and North Africa by stating that it "creates more problems than it solves, if any" (250). This may be true with respect to the social backlash spawned by the emergence of these groups, but Bradley's argument rests on a fundamental misunderstanding of human sexuality. He, in effect, equates male homosexuality to pedophilia, alleging that it is culturally permissible and claims that it "could be fairly described as universal" (242), particularly in Morocco. He says it is common for Moroccan men to engage in sexual acts with prepubescent boys as a means of preserving female purity until marriage (238-9). He holds that the practice of pederasty (referring to sex between a man and a boy), is relatively socially acceptable (238) and contends that the push for gay rights has inadvertently jeopardized the social acceptability of pederasty, as it "threaten[s] the peaceful social harmony" (243). He writes,

Pederasty in the Arab world remains as ubiquitous as the

call to prayer. So long as the sexual behavior is not spoken of publicly, it does not subvert existing homosocial norms, and it is not therefore perceived as a threat. The trick seems to be to not mention the subject in categorizable terms, not to acknowledge its existence if at all possible, and therefore not to have to deal with its distinct aspect of social reality. (243).

This implies that Bradley advocates for the LGBTQ+ community to stay in the closet in order to preserve the practice of pederasty. However, pederasty and/or pedophilia is *not* homosexuality, but is instead a form of child exploitation and abuse. Therefore, Bradley's argument is incorrect (and downright offensive) because it falsely equates the two.

Also, Bradley's view of homosexuality disregards the existence of lesbians and bisexuals altogether. Bradley's conception of homosexuality is a gross oversimplification and is blatantly derogatory to members of the LGBTQ+ community. Homosexuality refers to one's attraction to the same sex as well as the persistence of emotional and physical relationships between two consenting adults of the same sex. Feigning ignorance to the existence of queer people in the MENA—or attempting to minimize or erase them—in no way benefits them, as Bradley implies. In fact, a common goal of LGBTQ+ people in the MENA is to court international allies willing to signal boost their causes. Members of the LGBTQ+ community face severe discrimination in the MENA, and because of this reality, it is rational for them to engage in activism granted the opportunity to do so arrises. Homophobia and transphobia is so rampant that straight and cis people (perceived to be being gay or trans) are harmed by it as well. The social status quo in the region could, in theory, be disrupted by the presence of politically antagonistic LGBTQ+

activists, but that is not an inherently bad thing; in fact, it's their *goal*. Movements are inherently disruptive to necessitate social and political change. That is the very nature of social movements. LGBTQ+ rights are human rights, and Western observers have no right to tell queer people in the MENA their cause is too disruptive or unreasonable. They too deserve justice and equality like queer people around the world.

Homosexuality and gender dysphoria transcends culture. There is evidence both are innate, naturally occurring biological phenomena. Although culture is important in that it "provides guidelines or scripts for appropriate sexual responses" (Bancroft 2002, 19), cultural criterions for human sexuality does not detract from the plethora of evidence that suggests attraction to the same sex is an irreversible human characteristic and may occur for a number of reasons that are determined by fetal development (Blanchard 2000) or one's genetic predisposition (see Murphy 2005; Gavrilets & Rice 2009; O'Riordan 2012). With regard to gender identity, evidence shows there are underlying genetic and physiological factors that make people predisposed to be trans. Foreman et al. (2019) discovered an association between gender dysphoria and "several genes involved in sex hormone-signaling" that were "overrepresented in transgender women." Additionally, Flint et al. (2020) finds that transgender women have "brain-structural alterations that differ from their biological sex as well as their perceived gender" when compared to cisgender individuals, which suggests some people assigned male at birth (AMAB) can be naturally predisposed to be trans depending on the pattern of their brain structure. One can speculate that the same is true for trans men (assigned female at birth, or AFAB) and non-binary people (both AMAB and AFAB). These are just two of many studies confirming the innate nature of transness. While it is true gender is a social construct, biological phenomena ultimately determines whether an individual will assume characteristics that are masculine, feminine, both, or neither. Transgender and non-binary people, like cisgender people, tend to adopt their preferred gender identities in adolescence. Therefore, criticism from cultural relativists is unwarranted for the fact that being homosexual or trans is not a choice and will be just as prevalent in the Middle East and North Africa as it is in Western states regardless of restrictive cultural norms.

Whitaker (2006) states, "[a]rabs nowadays have just too much contact with the rest of the world to maintain an isolationist 'cultural purity' approach" (224) and adds that "exposure to foreign ideas and influences cannot be prevented" (212), which explains the popularity of the 'LGBTQ' acronym in the region. It is an acronym that maintains synonymity with the global queer community and encapsulates the totality of people participating in the worldwide movement for equality of sex and gender minorities, and queer Arabs want to be included in that global community of queer liberationists.[140]

Queer rights movements in the global South are equally legitimate to their Western counterparts, therefore social scientists should not be weary of having a "Western bias" when it comes to sex and gender issues in foreign cultures. Foreign queer rights movements should be included in social movement research. The

---

[140] This does not imply that there is a lack of diversity from a linguistic standpoint since each language has its own unique politically correct term(s) to describe gays and lesbians, such as "kuchu" in Uganda, or "mithli" and "mithliyya" for gay men and women in several MENA states (Whitaker 2006, 14), although this does vary. Nonetheless, most gay and trans Arab activists observed throughout the duration of this study self-identify with the 'LGBTQ' moniker, but cultural relativists still deny the universalization of LGBTQ+ rights.

geneses of these movements is transpiring at this very moment. Some LGBTQ+ rights movements in the region are in their Stonewall and post-Stonewall eras depending on the state. Some movements have already witnessed the rise of their own Marsha P. Johnsons and Sylvia Riveras. It would behoove social scientists to follow these social movements closely, as the queer activists of today are pioneers creating a blueprint for the social movements of tomorrow. Studying them will provide insight into how controversial causes evolve into robust social movements in the era of technology.

Conclusion

The internet should be scrupulously examined in authoritarian regimes across the globe in order to develop insight into other potential ways activists are utilizing it to pressure governments and push their causes. As access to the internet increases, so too will the size of these movements. Though the scope of this study is limited to three case studies, the applicability of the internet mobilization hypothesis is not restricted to Morocco, Algeria, and Tunisia, nor the aggregate MENA region. Colombant (2010) reports that LGBTQ+ activists in many Sub-Saharan African countries are also employing online strategies to combat social and legal discrimination. This is evident in Uganda, but is also applicable to the Russian LGBTQ+ movement as well. For this reason, I believe my methodology will prove useful for assessing the catalyst(s) of these movements and what determines their overall strength in other authoritarian states throughout the world.

The explanatory power of the internet mobilization hypothesis could potentially extend beyond LGBTQ+ movements.

It may also prove useful for other types of socially unacceptable movements for postmaterialist causes such as atheist, agnostic, areligious, anti-theist, and deist (AAAAD) movements seeing as how they are equally vilified, especially in highly religious countries, thus making the internet a necessity for mobilization of their communities as well. Sectarian, religious and ethnic minorities could also utilize the internet for political mobilization in the same way queer people do in the MENA. Social movements that would otherwise not exist could soon be materializing around the globe due to the internet. Increased access to the internet coupled with a rise in global authoritarianism makes this social movement research particularly necessary and urgent.

All types of activists—both material and postmaterial—have used the internet to facilitate collective action and pressure regimes. Various types of episodic movements around the globe have also been instigated online, including small-scale anti-military protests in Russia to large-scale revolutions which lead to the ousting of dictatorial leaders in the Arab spring (Lonkila 2008; Lynch 2012; Lust 2013). Implications of the internet on culture, religion, and governance can only be speculated, but its impact on social movements is evident.

Although the MENA is heterogenous, citizens of states in this region are rational actors that are no less likely than anyone else to aspire to attain freedom and equality in society. One's decision to engage in a pursuit to impact public policy will not ensue unless the proper conditions—namely, adequate access to the internet—are sufficient since it is not pragmatic for advocates of controversial causes to engage in activism without anonymity.

The notion of a 'clash of civilizations' is questionable in an era of globalization and expanded access to new technology. Although there are cultural, religious, and linguistic differences with respect to sexual orientation and gender identity, the inclination of cultural relativists to peg emerging postmaterialist causes as Western phenomena is not grounded in logic, nor is it empirically or factually verifiable. Instead, these movements have been delayed in the MENA not because gay and transgender people do not exist there or because they want to emulate the West, but because they have not had access to a viable political resource—the internet—until recently. This argument strengthens resource mobilization theory and emphasizes the importance of political opportunities in the emergence of new social movements.

Like-minded and marginalized individuals are coming together throughout the region to improve their social status and stake their claim in politics. LGBTQ+ activism in the Middle East and North Africa is not going anywhere, but the question rather is how much momentum these movements will gain in the near future considering how big they have become given the short period of time they have existed. Political scientists contend that the Arab uprising, an extraordinary political phenomenon, transpired due to access to new technology (Lust 2013; Lynch 2012; Hussain & Howard 2013). The internet was cited as a key tool for Arab activists seeing that it was useful for mass political mobilization in 2011 (Lust 2013, 283). This book demonstrates that the internet can catalyze other types of activism as well: gay and transgender equality movements. The political landscape in the Middle East and North Africa will likely continue to transform due to the increasing prominence of the internet.

Acknowledgments

I am very thankful and privileged to have had the opportunity to work with the faculty at Portland State University's Mark O. Hatfield School of Government. I am particularly appreciative of Dr. Lindsay Benstead and Dr. Melodi Valdini for acting as my mentors and assisting me throughout the course of this book's development. I am also grateful to Dr. Albert Spencer III primarily for being an influential figure to me during my time as an undergraduate. Furthermore I want to thank Dr. David Kinsella along with Dr. Benstead and Dr. Valdini again for their willingness to participate in the defense of my Master's thesis. Their recommendation to publish my thesis—either into a journal article or a book—and continue my research was confirmation that it has produced insightful results. All of my professors have been instrumental in both my personal development and academic success throughout my tenure as a graduate student and I am very grateful to them for that.

Glossary

Cisgender - Is an individual whose birth sex correlates with their prescribed gender. In essence it is an individual that does not identify as transgender or agender.

Coming Out - The process by which an individual publicly reveals a fundamental component of their identity (e.g. sexual, gender, religious, secular, feminist, etc.).

Code Switching - When a gay person temporarily adopts masculine/feminine body language and mannerisms consistent with traditional gender norms in order to pass as heterosexual in public. Code switching is used in non-LGBTQ+ contexts as well by other marginalized groups.

Gay Community - Though this has homosexual connotations, it is typically used as an umbrella term that is inclusive of the collective LGBTQ community, including transgender individuals, asexual individuals, pansexuals, intersex persons, and even straight allies.

Gender - Is different from sex in that sex refers to one's physiological composition, whereas gender is typically the expression of masculine, feminine, or neither of those two characteristics. Descriptively, men usually choose to express their gender by being masculine while women express it by being more feminine. Though this may be a prevalent cultural norm, it is purely stereotypical. Many individuals deviate from these traditional gender roles, hence the need for descriptive terms such as "tom boy," for example.

Gender Identity - Refers to how individuals express their gender or label themselves.

Gender Minority - Is an individual or group of individuals that are not cisgender; that is, their birth sex does not match their gender (see Transgender definition).

Intersectionality - Is when one person has multiple identities. For example, an individual may be a member of multiple communities (e.g. gay woman of color, straight cisgender secular man, or Islamic feminist). The labels most individuals identify with are not mutually exclusive.

LGBTQIA+ - An acronym referring to the aggregate community of sexual and gender minorities; lesbian, gay, bisexual, transgender, and queer/questioning, intersex and asexual individuals. Several variants are possible such as 'LGBTI' or 'LGBTP' to include intersex and pansexual individuals.

MENA - Is an acronym that refers to states within the Middle East and North African region. It is also commonly referred to as the "Arab world."

Non-Binary Gender Identity - Is a gender identity that is not associated with the male or female sex. A non-binary gender identity may incorporate characteristics from both the male and female genders or may deviate from both entirely. It is a gender identity that is more flexible and not subject to normative preconceptions of the binary gender system.

Sexual Minority - Is an individual that is attracted to the same sex or gender, is not attracted to binary genders, or does not have a sexual orientation altogether.

Transgender - A person that identifies as a gender not correlated with the sex they were assigned at birth.

Two-Spirit - A term used by indigenous people that identify with both the masculine and feminine genders. (Also referred to as '2Spirit' or '2S').

List of Tables

List of Figures

Figure 3.1

Figure 4.1

Figure 6.1

Figure 6.2

Figure 6.3

Figure 6.4

Figure 6.5

References

Abedine, Saad and Elizabeth Landau. 2014. "Ugandan Tabloid Prints List of 'Homosexuals'." *CNN*. 25 February, 2014. Web. (Accessed: 24 March, 2015). <http://www.cnn.com/2014/02/25/world/africa/uganda-anti-gay-law/>.

Abu Nawas. "About Us! A Rebrique for us Connetr." Web. (Accessed: 25 March, 2015). <http://abunawas-algerie.e-monsite.com/pages/qui-sommes-nous-une-rebrique-pour-nous-connetre.html>.

Achi, George. 2009. "Peaceful Rally in Beirut for Gay Rights." *Monthly Review*. 23 February, 2009. Web. (Accessed: 27 March, 2015). <http://mrzine.monthlyreview.org/2009/achi230209.html>.

Afrol News. 2010. "Algerian Gays Lit Candles for Recognition." 13 October, 2010. Web. (Accessed: 25 March, 2015). <http://www.afrol.com/articles/36770>.

Al Arabiya News. 2013. "Lawyer: Two Moroccans Jailed for Homosexuality." 21 May, 2013. Web. (Accessed: 25 March, 2015). <http://english.alarabiya.net/en/News/middle-east/2013/05/21/Lawyer-Two-Moroccans-jailed-for-homosexuality-.html>.

———. 2014. "Tunisian Police Disperse Islamic Protestors." 12 April, 2014. Web. (Accessed: 6 May, 2015). <http://english.alarabiya.net/en/News/2014/04/12/Calm-returns-after-Tunisian-Salafist-protest.html>.

Alexa. 2015a. "Top Sites in Morocco." *Alexa Internet, Incorporated.* Web. (Accessed: 8 May, 2015). <http://www.alexa.com/topsites/countries/MA>.

———. 2015b. "Top Sites in Algeria." *Alexa Internet, Incorporated.* Web. (Accessed: 8 May, 2015). <http://www.alexa.com/topsites/countries;0/DZ>.

Alizadeh, Hossein. 2014. "When Coming Out Is a Death Sentence: The Rising Tide of Violence Against LGBT Iraqis." *The Huffington Post.* 26 November, 2014. Web. (Accessed: 20 March, 2015). <http://www.huffingtonpost.com/hossein-alizadeh/when-coming-out-is-a-deat_b_6201210.html>.

Al Jazeera. 2013. "Salafist Group Clashes With Police in Tunisia." 20 May, 2013. Web. (Accessed: 6 May, 2015). <http://www.aljazeera.com/news/africa2013/05/20 135198155650292.html>.

Alturi. 2020. "False marriage claims in Tunisia have led to anti-LGBT+ attacks." *Gay Star News.* 4 May 2020. Web. (Accessed: 19 November 2023). <https://www.alturi.org/news_items/false-marriage-claims-in-tunisia-have-led-to-anti-lgbt-attacks-04-may-2020/>.

Amand, Jason. 2012. "Lebanese LGBT Group Protests Against Gay Anal Testing." *Edge Media Network.* 16 August, 2012. Web. (Accessed: 27 March, 2015). <http://www.edgeboston.com/news/international/news/136092lebanese_lgbt_group_protests_against_gay_anal_te sting>.

Asmelash, Leah and Brian Ries. 2019. "This Tunisian lawyer is hoping to be the country's first openly gay president." *CNN.* 9 April, 2019. Web. (Accessed: 1 April, 2024). <https://www.cnn.com/2019/08/09/world/mounir-baatour-tunisia-president-candidate-trnd/index.html>.

Associated Press. 2022. "Kuwait court overturns law criminalizing transgender people." February 17, 2022. Web. (Accessed: March 26, 2024). <https://apnews.com/article/middle-east-dubai-united-arab-emirates-kuwait-19f74a75f740e7495b7a809a650 67f44>.

Arab Barometer. 2018-2019. "Acceptance of homosexuality (Arab Countries). Web. (Accessed: 14 November 2023). <https://www.equaldex.com/surveys/acceptance-of-homosexuality-arab-barometer>.

Association Alouen. "Our Mission." Web. (Accessed: 25 March, 2015). <http://alouen.org/notre-mission/>.

———. 2011. "Kif-Kif: Une Association Qui a Su Briser les Tabous." 10 October, 2011. Web. (Accessed: 7 May, 2015). <http://alouen.org/kif-kif-une-association-qui-a-su-briser-les-tabous/>.

AWID. 2016. "Tunisia: Suspension of the activities of the LGBT rights association Shams." *Association for Women's Rights and Development.* 13 January 2016. Web. (Accessed via The Wayback Machine: 19 November 2023). <https://web.archive.org/web/20170418223152/https:// www.awid.org/get-involved/tunisia-suspension-activities-lgbt-rights-association-shams>.

Bagri, Neha Thirani. 2017. "Everyone treated me like a saint"—In Iran, there's only one way to survive as a transgender person." *Quartz.* 19 April, 2017. Web. (Accessed: March 7, 2024).

<https://qz.com/889548/everyone-treated-me-like-a-saint-in-iran-theres-only-one-way-to-survive-as-a-transgender-person>.

Bancroft, John. 2002. "Biological Factors in Human Sexuality." *The Journal of Sex Research* 39 (1): 15-21.

Bayat, Asef. 2000. "Social Movements, Activism and Social Development in the Middle East." United Nations. *United Nations Research Institute for Social Development*, Programme Paper Number 3. Web. (Accessed: 6 May, 2015). <http://www.unrisd.org/80256b3c005bccf9/(httpauxpages)/9c2befd0ee1c73b380 256b5e004ce4c3/$file/bayat.pdf>.

———. 2002. "Activism and Social Development in the Middle East." *International Journal of Middle East Studies* 34 (1): 1-28.

———. 2005. "Islamism and Social Movement Theory." *Third World Quarterly* 26 (6): 891-908.

BBC. 2014. "Where is it illegal to be gay?" *BBC News*. 10 February, 2014. Web. (Accessed: 20 March, 2015). <http://www.bbc.com/news/world-25927595>.

BBC. 2024. "Tunisia: Is democracy there being destroyed?" *BBC News*. 20 April, 2023. Web. (Accessed: 14 November, 2023). <https://www.bbc.com/news/worldeurope-65125593>.

Belonksy, Andrew. 2008. "Moroccan Paper Fined for 'Sexual Perversion' Smear." *Queerty*. 25 March, 2008. Web. (Accessed: 25 March, 2015). <http://www.queerty.com/moroccan-paper-fined-for-sexual-perversion-smear-20080325>.

Belson, David. 2014. "State of the Internet." *Akamai* 7(4): 1-62. Web. (Accessed: 7 May, 2015). <http://www.akamai.com/dl/content/q4-2014-soti-report.pdf>.

Beresford, Meka. 2017. "Gay actor attacked after director told fans on Facebook to rape him." *Pink News.* 28 August 2017. Web. (Accessed: 18 November, 2023). <https://www.thepinknews.com/2017/08/28/gay-actor-attacked-after-director-told-fans-on-facebook-to-rape-him/>.

Bergen, Peter and Alec Reynolds. 2005. "Blowback Revisited: Today's Insurgents in Iraq Are Tomorrow's Terrorists." *Foreign Affairs* 84 (6): 2-6.

Blackshaw, Anna. 2012. "After the Arab Spring, the Future is Uncertain for Muslim Gay Youth." *Indy Week.* 19 September, 2012. Web. (Accessed: 25 March, 2015). <http://www.indyweek.com/indyweek/after-the-arab-spring-the-future-is-uncertain-for-muslim-gay-youth/Content?oid=3152028>.

Blanchard, Ray. 2000. "Fraternal Birth Order, Maternal Immune Reactions, and Homosexuality in Men." *Politics and the Life Sciences* 19 (2): 157-159.

Boudjadi, Kamel. 2010. "Gay Imam Gets Two-Year Jail Sentence in Algeria." *San Diego Gay & Lesbian News.* 14 April, 2010. Web. (Accessed: 25 March, 2015). <http://www.sdgln.com/news/2010/04/14/gay-imam-gets-two-year-jail-sentence-algeria#sthash.n7CKHr9h.dpbs>.

Bradley, John. 2010. *Behind the Veil of Vice: The Business and Culture of Sex in the Middle East.* New York: Palgrave Macmillan.

Buechler, Steven. 1995. "New Social Movement Theories." *The Sociological Quarterly* 36 (3): 441-464.

Canning, Paul. 2011. "Tunisian Islamists Offer Reassurance to Gays, Women, Drinkers." *Care2*. 25 October, 2011. Web. (Accessed: 24 March 2015). <http://www.care2.com/causes/tunisian-islamists-offer-reassurance-to-gays-women-drinkers.html>.

Flint, Class, Katharina Förster, Sophie A. Koser, Carsten Konrad, Pienie Zwitserlood, Klaus Berger, Marco Hermesdorf, Tilo Kircher, Igor Nenadic, Axel Krug, Bernhard T. Baune, Katharina Dohm, Ronny Redlick, Nils Opel, Volker Arolt, Tim Hahn, Xiaoyi Jiang, Udo Dannlowski and Dominik Grotegerd. 2020. "Biological sex classification with structural MRI data shows increased misclassification in transgender women." *Neuropsychopharmacology* 45(1758-1765). Web. (Accessed: 16 March, 2024). <https://www.nature.com/articles/s41386-020-0666-3>.

Celik, Fatima. 2021. "Turkey: LGBT+ endure attacks amid Erdogan reign." *Deutsche Welle (DW)*. 16 March 2021. Web. (Accessed: 15 November 2023). <https://www.dw.com/en/turkeys-lgbt-endure-brutal-attacks-amid-erdogan-reign/a-56891497>.

Charrad, Mounira. 2001. *States and Women's Rights: The Making of Postcolonial Tunisia, Algeria, and Morocco*. Berkeley: University of California Press.

CIA World Factbook. 2014a. "Country Comparison: Internet Users." United States. Central Intelligence Agency. Web. (Accessed: 24 March, 2015). <https://www.cia.gov/library/publications/the-world-factbook/rankorder/2153rank.html>.

———. 2014b. "Country Comparison: Population." United States. Central Intelligence Agency. Web. (Accessed: 24 March, 2015).

<https://www.cia.gov/library/publications/the-world-factbook/rankorder/2119rank.html>.

———. 2014c. "Country Comparison: HIV/AIDS - Adult Prevalence Rate." United States. Central Intelligence Agency. Web. (Accessed: 24 March, 2015). <https://www.cia.gov/library/publications/the-world-factbook/rankorder/2155rank.html>.

______. 2014d. "Africa: Algeria." United States. Central Intelligence Agency. Web. (Accessed: 7 May, 2015). <https://www.cia.gov/library/publications/the-world-factbook/geos/ag.html>.

______. 2022. "Internet Users. United States. Central Intelligence Agency. Web. (Accessed: 10 March, 2024). <https://www.cia.gov/the-world-factbook/about/archives/2022/field/internet-users/>.

Cohen, Dudi. 2011. "Gay Community in Iran Launches Facebook Campaign Against Regime that Views Their Sexual Identity a Crime Punishable by Death." *Y Net News*. 12 September, 2011. Web. (Accessed: 28 March, 2015). <http://www.ynetnews.com/articles/0,7340,L-4121043,00.html>.

Colombant, Nico. 2010. "Africa's Gay Activists Use Internet to Advance Homosexual Rights." *Voice of America*. 14 June, 2010. Web. (Accessed: 8 May, 2015). <http://www.voanews.com/content/africas-gay-activists-use-internet-to-advance-homosexual-rights—96381899/154893.html>.

Cordall, Simon Speakman. 2019. "Meet the man hoping to become the Muslim world's first openly gay president." *Independent*. 16 July, 2019. Web. (Accessed: 1 April, 2024).

<https://www.independent.co.uk/news/world/middle-east/
tunisia-lgbt-gay-president-candidate-mounir-baatour-
shams-a9003656.html>.

Dahl, Robert. 1971. *Polyarchy; Participation and Opposition.*
New Haven: Yale University Press.

______1989. Democracy and Its Critics. New Haven: Yale
University Press.

Damon, Arwa and Zeynep Bilginsoy. 2015. "Amid Brazen,
Deadly Attacks, Gay Syrians Tell of Fear of ISIS
Persecution." *CNN.* 6 March, 2015. Web. (Accessed: 20
March, 2015).
<http://www.cnn.com/2015/03/05/middleeast/isis-lgbt-
persecution/>.

Data Reportal. 2020. "Digital 2020: Palestine." 18 February, 2020.
Web. (Accessed: 10 March 2024).
<https://datareportal.com/reports/digital-2020-palestine>.

Davies, James. 1962. "Toward a Theory of Revolution." *American
Sociological Review* 27 (1): 5-19.

Dehghan, Saeed. 2012. "Iran's Persecution of Gay Community
Revealed." *The Guardian.* 17 May, 2012. Web. (Accessed:
28 March, 2015).
<http://www.theguardian.com/world/2012/may/17/iran-
persecution-gay-community-revealed>.

Ebel, Francesca. 2021. "Tunisia: LGBT Activist's assault by
police seen as a pattern." *Associated Press.* 10 December,
2021. Web. (Accessed: 18 November, 2021).
<https://apnews.com/article/coronavirus-pandemic-
business-health-africa-tunisia-f3d0629969ed647f9
eab2b4465f14d70>.

Encyclopedia Britannica, Inc. 2008. "Postmaterialism."
Dictionary.com. Web. (Accessed: 16 March, 2015).

<http://dictionary.reference.com/browse/postmaterialism>.

eMarketer. 2013. "Smartphone Usage to Nearly Double in the Middle East and Africa." 1 October, 2013. Web. (Accessed: 7 May, 2015). <http://www.emarketer.com/Article/Smartphone-Usage-Nearly-Double-Middle-East-Africa/1010249>.

Eremenko, Alexey. 2013. "Iranian Atheists: Waiting to Come Out." *Sputnik*. 19 March, 2013. Web. (Accessed: 28 March, 2015). <http://sputniknews.com/analysis/20130319/180108 603.html>.

Falk, Pamela. 2014. "LGBT rights 45 years after the Stonewall riots." *CBS News*. 27 June, 2014. Web. (Accessed: 23 March, 2015). <http://www.cbsnews.com/news/lgbt-rights-45-years-after-the-stonewall-riots/>.

Feder, J. Lester. 2014. "LGBT Egyptians Go Into Hiding As Regime Cracks Down." *Buzzfeed*. 23 September, 2014. Web. (Accessed: 29 March, 2015). <http://www.buzzfeed.com/lesterfeder/why-egypts-regime-has-launched-a-mass- crackdown-on-lgbt-righ#.rpvnJ1bkb>.

Financial Mirror. 2022. "Cyprus introduces gender change legislation." *Financial Mirror*. 30 September 2022. Web. (Accessed: 15 November 2023). <https://www.financialmirror.com/2022/09/30/cyprus-introduces-gender-change-legislation/>.

Fisher, Max. 2012. "Photos of Clandestine Gay Rights Rally in Tehran." *The Atlantic*. 22 May, 2012. Web. (Accessed: 28 March, 2015).

<http://www.theatlantic.com/international/archive/ 2012/05/photos-of-a-clandestine-gay-rights-rally-in-tehran/257500/#slide9>.

Foreman, Madeleine, Lauren Hare, Kate York, Kara Balakrishnan, Francisco J. Sánchez, Fintan Harte, Jaco Erasmus, Eric Vilain and Vincent R. Harley. "Genetic Link Between Gender Dysphoria and Sex Hormone Signaling." *The Journal of Clinical Endocrinology & Metabolism* 104 (2): 390-396. Web. (Accessed: 16 March, 2024). <https://pubmed.ncbi.nlm.nih.gov/30247609/>.

Freedom House. 2005. "Freedom in the World: Morocco." Web. (Accessed: 8 May, 2015). <https://freedomhouse.org/report/freedom-world/ 2005morocco#.VUwz0b64ldg>.

———. 2011. "Freedom on the Net: Tunisia." Web. (Accessed: 8 May, 2015). <https://freedomhouse.org/report/freedom-net/2011/ tunisia#.VT_kar64ldg>.

———. 2013. "Freedom in the World: Algeria." Web. (Accessed: 8 May, 2015). <https://freedomhouse.org/report/freedom-world/2013/ algeria#.VUw4dr64ldg>.

———. 2014. "Freedom on the Net." Web. (Accessed: 8 May, 2015). <http://freedomhouse.org/report/freedom-net/freedom-net-2014#.VT_jvb64ldi>.

———. 2015. "Freedom in the World 2015." Web. (Accessed: 6 May, 2015). <https://freedomhouse.org/report/freedom-world/freedom-world-2015#.VRTs1L64ldg>.

________. 2022a. "Freedom on the Net 2022: Tunisia." Web. (Accessed: 19 November 2022). <https://freedomhouse.org/country/tunisia/freedom-net/2022>.

________. 2022b. "Freedom on the Net 2022: Morocco." Web. (Accessed: 19 November 2022). <https://freedomhouse.org/country/morocco/freedom-net/2022>.

________. 2023a. "Freedom on the Net 2023: Morocco." Web. (Accessed: 19 November 2022). <https://freedomhouse.org/country/morocco/freedom-net/2023>.

________. 2023b. "Freedom in the World 2023: Algeria." Web. (Accessed: 12, January 2024). <https://freedomhouse.org/country/algeria/freedom-world/2023>.

Galal, Saifaddin. 2023a."Internet penetration rate in Morocco from 2017 to 2023." *Statista*. 26 April 2023. Web. (Accessed: 19 November 2023). <https://www.statista.com/statistics/1172770/internet-penetration-rate-morocco/>.

Galal, Saifaddin. 2023b. "Internet usage in Algeria - statistics & facts." 21 December, 2023. Web. (Accessed: 12 January, 2024). <https://www.statista.com/topics/10163/internet-usage-in-algeria/#topicOverview>.

Gavrilets, Sergey and William Rice. 2009. "Genetic Models of Homosexuality: Generating Testable Predictions." *Proceedings: Biological Sciences* 273 (1605): 3031-3038.

GME (Gay Middle East). 2004. "Syria: Cleric Saves Transexual." *Gay Middle East*. 3 May 2004. Web. (Accessed via Wayback Machine: 15 November, 2023). <https://web.archive.org/web/20110711080616/http://www.gaymiddleeast.com/news/article17.htm>.

Gettleman, Jeffrey. 2011. "Ugandan Who Spoke Up for Gays Is Beaten to Death." *The New York Times*. 21 January, 2011. Web. (Accessed: 23 March, 2015). <http://www.nytimes.com/2011/01/28/world/africa/28uganda.html?_r=0>.

Ghanmi, Lamine. 2010. "Morocco Resists Islamist Calls to Ban Elton John." *Reuters*. 17 May, 2010. Web. (Accessed: 24 March, 2015). <http://www.reuters.com/article/2010/05/17/us-eltonjohn-idUSTRE64G5DV20100517>.

Goodman, Melvin. 2013. "The Blowback from Interventionism." *Consortium News*. 27 April, 2013. Web. (Accessed: 23 March, 2015). <https://consortiumnews.com/2013/04/27/the-blowback-from-interventionism/>.

Gray, Stephen. 2012. "Casablanca: Gay Cruise Diverted." *Pink News*. 2 July, 2012. Web. (Accessed: 25 March, 2015). <http://www.pinknews.co.uk/2012/07/02/casablanca-gay-cruise-diverted/>.

Grez, Matias. 2023. "BBC Apologizes for report's 'inappropriate' question to Morocco women's team captain." *CNN Sports*. 25 July, 2023. Web. (Accessed: 18 November 2023). <https://www.cnn.com/2023/07/24/football/bbc-apologizes-inappropriate-question-ghizlane-chebbak-spt-intl/index.html>.

Grew, Tony. 2008. "Moroccan Newspaper Sued by Judges Over Gay Party Story." *Pink News*. 26 March, 2008. Web. (Accessed: 25 March, 2008). <http://www.pinknews.co.uk/2008/03/26/moroccan-newspaper-sued-by-judges-over-gay-party-story/>.

GSMA. 2014. "The Mobile Economy: Arab States 2014." *Groupe Speciale Mobile Association*. Web. (Accessed: 7 May, 2015). <http://arabstates.gsmamobileeconomy.com/GSMA_ME_Arab_States_2014.pdf>.

Hafften, Marie. 2012. "Lesbians in Morocco: Should We Stay or Should We Go?" *Global Post*. 22 June, 2012. Web. (Accessed: 25 March, 2015). <http://www.globalpost.com/dispatch/news/regions/africa/morocco/120621/morocco-LGBT-gay-lesbian>.

Harb, Imad K. "Algeria Reestablishes Authoritarianism through Elections." *Arab Center Washington DC*. 1 July, 2021. Wed. (Accessed: 19 November 2023). <https://arabcenterdc.org/resource/algeria-reestablishes-authoritarianism-through-elections/>.

Harim, O. 2014. "Behind the Scenes With Algeria's First LGBT Magazine. *The Observers*. 12 March, 2014. Web. (Accessed: 26 March, 2015). <http://observers.france24.com/content/20141203-algeria-first-lgbt-magazine-gay>.

Harit, Fouad. 2013. "Maroc: Une Cyber-Campagne Contre L'Homophobie." *Afrik*. 17 May, 2013. Web. (Accessed: 25 March, 2015). <http://www.afrik.com/maroc-une-cyber-campagne-contre-l-homophobie>.

Hassan Al-Ashraf, Rabat. 2009. "Gay Seminar Stirs Outrage in Morocco." *Al Arabiya News*. 19 March, 2009. Web. (Accessed: 25 March, 2015). <http://www.alarabiya.net/articles/2009/03/19/68776.html>.

Hayoun, Massoud. 2014a. "Morocco Convicts Six Men for Homosexuality." *Al Jazeera America*. 15 May, 2014. Web. (Accessed: 25 March, 2015). <http://america.aljazeera.com/articles/2014/5/15/morocco-convicts6menforhomosexualityamidnationaldialogueongays.html>.

———. 2014b. "Moroccans' Gay Pride March Aims to Carve Out New Space From a Distance." *Al Jazeera America*. 26 June, 2015. Web. (Accessed: 25 March, 2015). <http://america.aljazeera.com/articles/2014/6/26/morocco-gay-pride0.html>.

Helem. 2014. "About Us." Web. (Accessed: 31 March, 2015). <http://helem.net/?q=node/59>.

Hopkins, Curt. 2012. "Tunisia Promises to End Internet Censorship." *The Daily Dot*. 14 September, 2012. Web. (Accessed: 8 May, 2015). <http://www.dailydot.com/news/tunisia-internet-censorship/>.

Hubbard, Ben. 2015. "Caning of Saudi Blogger is Delayed Amid Protests." *The New York Times*. 16 January, 2015. Web. (Accessed: 16 March, 2015). <http://www.nytimes.com/2015/01/17/world/caning-of-saudi-blogger-is-delayed-amid-protests.html?_r=0>.

Huffington Post. 2015. "Tunisia's New Gay Rights Fight." 13 March, 2015. Web. (Accessed: 25 March, 2015).

<http://www.huffingtonpost.com/2014/12/11/tunisia-gay-rights_n_6304872.html>.

Human Rights Watch. 2020. "Algeria: Mass Convictions for Homosexuality." 15 October, 2020. Web. (Accessed: 12 January, 2024). <https://www.hrw.org/news/2020/10/15/algeria-mass-convictions-homosexuality#:~:text=(Beirut)%20%20An%20Algerian%20court,Hu man%20Rights%20Watch%20said%20today.>.

Hussain, Muzammil and Philip Howard. 2013. "What Best Explains Successful Protest Cascades? ICTs and the Fuzzy Causes of the Arab Spring." *International Studies Review* 15 (1): 48-66. Index on Censorship. 2005. "Dossier on Morocco." *Index on Censorship* 34 (3): 154-165.

Icotza. 2016. "Tunisia: Court annuls the suspension of LGBTI organization." *Frontline Defenders*. 25 February, 2016. Web. (Accessed: 19 November 2013). <https://www.frontlinedefenders.org/en/tunisia-court-annuls-suspension-lgbti-organisation-shams>.

Inglehart, Ronald. 1977. *The Silent Revolution: Changing Values and Political Styles Among Western Publics.* Princeton, New Jersey: Princeton University Press.

———. 1990. *Culture Shift in Advanced Industrial Society.* Princeton, New Jersey: Princeton University Press.

Internet World Stats. 2012a. "Morocco: Internet Usage and Marketing Report." Web. (Accessed: 7 May, 2015). <http://www.internetworldstats.com/af/ma.htm>.

———. 2012b. "Algeria: Internet Usage and Marketing Report." Web. (Accessed: 7 May, 2015). <http://www.internetworldstats.com/af/dz.htm>.

———. 2012c. "Tunisia: Internet Usage and Marketing Report."

Web. (Accessed: 7 May, 2015).
<http://www.internetworldstats.com/af/tn.htm>.
———. 2014. "Internet Usage Statistics for Africa." Web.
(Accessed: 26 March, 2015).
<http://www.internetworldstats.com/stats1.htm>.
Iranian Queer Organization. 2015a. "Our Story." Web. (Accessed:
28 March, 2015).
<http://www.irqo.org/english/?page_id=389>.
Itaborahy, Lucas and Jingshu Zhu. 2014. "State-Sponsored
Homophobia: A World Survey of Laws: Criminalisation,
Protection and Recognition of Same-Sex Love."
*International Lesbian Gay Bisexual Trans and Intersex
Association*. Web. (Accessed: 20 March, 2015).
<http://old.ilga.org/Statehomophobia/ILGA_SSHR
_2014_Eng.pdf>.
Iyengar, Shanto, Mark D. Peters, and Donald R. Kinder. 1993.
"Experimental Demonstrations of the 'Not-So-Minimal'
Consequences of Television News Program." In
Experimental Foundations of Political Science. Eds.
Donald R. Kinder and Thomas R. Palfrey. Michigan: The
University of Michigan Press.
Jasper, James. 1997. *The Art of Moral Protest: Culture,
Biography, and Creativity in Social Movements*. Chicago:
University of Chicago Press.
Jao, Ariel. 2018. "LGBTQ activists in Mideast, North Africa
speak out in new video project." *NBC News*. 25 April,
2018. Web. (Accessed: 18 November 2023).
<https://www.nbcnews.com/feature/nbc-out/lgbtq-
activists-mideast-north-africa-speak-out-new-video-
project-n868461>.

Jean-Jacques, Sarah. 2014. "Gay & Lesbian Mobilization in Algeria: The Emergence of a Movement." *Muftah*. 15 December, 2014. Web. (Accessed: 25 March, 2014). <http://muftah.org/gay-and-lesbian-mobilization-in-algeria/#.VRM19b64ldg>.

Joffé, George. 2014. "To Reign or Rule: Morocco's Halting Road to Liberalization." *World Politics Review*. 22 April, 2014. Web. (Accessed: 7 May, 2015). <http://www.worldpoliticsreview.com/articles/13719/to-reign-or-rule-morocco-s-halting-road-to-liberalization>.

Kanso, Heba. 2017. "Tunisia's first LGBTQ radio station keeps playing despite threats." *Reuters*. 27 December 2017. Web. (Accessed: 19 November 2023). <https://www.reuters.com/article/us-tunisa-gay-radio-idUSKBN1EL1HB/>.

Karimi, Faith and Nick Thompson. 2014. "Uganda's President Museveni Signs Controversial Anti-Gay Bill into Law." *CNN*. 25 February, 2014. Web. (Accessed: 23 March, 2015). <http://www.cnn.com/2014/02/24/world/africa/uganda-anti-gay-bill/>.

Kelmty - Associations Gays et Lesbiennes Tunisiens. 2015. *Facebook*. Web.(Accessed: 24 March, 2015). <http://www.facebook.com/kelmty>.

Kemp, Simon. 2022. "Digital 2022: Tunisia." *DataReportal*. 15 February 2022. Web. (Accessed: 19 November 2023). < https://datareportal.com/reports/digital-2022-tunisia>.

Khlifi, Roua. 2015. "Controversy in Tunisia over new gay association." *The Arab Weekly*. 12 June 2015. Web. (Accessed via The Wayback Machine: 19 November 2023).

<https://web.archive.org/web/20170829120719/http://
www.thearabweekly.com//?id=735>.

Kingsley, Patrick. 2014. "Egypt Jails Eight Men After 'Gay
Marriage' Ceremony on Nile." *The Guardian.* 3
November, 2014. Web. (Accessed: 16 March, 2015).
<http://www.theguardian.com/world/2014/nov/03/egypt-
jails-eight-men-gay-marriage-ceremony-nile>.

Kuhanen, Jan. 2008. "The Historiography of HIV and AIDS in
Uganda." *History in Africa* 35: 301-325.

Lee, Ian, and Sarah Sirgany. 2015. "Living in Fear: Egypt's Gay
Community." *CNN.* 2 January, 2015. Web. (Accessed: 29
March, 2015).
<http://www.cnn.com/2014/12/09/world/africa/egypts-
gay-community-living-in-fear/>.

Lee, Timothy. 2013. "Here's How Iran Censors the Internet." *The
Washington Post.* 15 August, 2013. Web. (Accessed: 28
March, 2015)
<http://www.washingtonpost.com/blogs/the-switch/wp/
2013/08/15/heres-how-iran-censors-the-internet/>.

Littauer, Dan. 2012. "Tunisian Human Rights Minister: No Free
Speech for Gays." *Pink News.* 6 February, 2012. Web.
(Accessed: 24 March, 2015).
<http://www.pinknews.co.uk/2012/02/06/tunisian-human-
rights-minister-no-free-speech-for-gays/>.

———. 2013. "Lebanon: Activists Protest Against Arrest and
Abuse of Gays." *Gay Star News.* 1 May, 2013. Web.
(Accessed: 27 March, 2015).
<http://www.gaystarnews.com/article/lebanon-activi
sts-protest-against-arrest-and-abuse-gays010513>.

———. 2014. "Lebanon Launches Police Raids Targeting Gay Men." *San Diego Gay & Lesbian News*. 15 August, 2014. Web. (Accessed: 27 March, 2015). <http://www.sdgln.com/news/2014/08/15/lebanon-launches-police-raidstargeting-gay-men#sthash.GuXXx5su.dpbs>.

Lonkila, Markku. 2008. "The Internet and Anti-Military Activism in Russia." *Europe-Asia Studies* 60 (7): 1125-1149.

Lucas, Michael. 2012. "Gays In The New, Complicated Tunisia." *Advocate*. 4 December, 2012. Web. (Accessed: 25 March, 2015). <http://www.advocate.com/commentary/2012/12/04/gays-new-and-complicated-tunisia>.

Lust, Ellen. 2013. *The Middle East*. 13th ed. Thousand Oaks, California: CQ Press.

Lutterback, Derek. 2013. "Tunisia After Ben Ali: Retooling the Tools of Oppression?" *Norwegian Peacebuilding Resource Centre.* Web. (Accessed: 6 May, 2015). <http://www.peacebuilding.no/var/ezflow_site/storage/original/application/8a4a01231edc1bc44e19af11823 14d46.pdf>.

Lynch, Mark. 2012. *The Arab Uprising: The Unfinished Revolutions of the New Middle East.* 1st ed. New York: Public Affairs.

Marks, Gary. 2009. "Modernization Theory and Changes Over Time in the Reproduction of Socioeconomic Inequalities in Australia." *Social Forces* 88 (2): 917-944.

Marzouki, Nadia. 2010. "Algeria" in *Women's Rights in the Middle East and North Africa: Progress Amid Resistance.* Eds. Sanja Kelly and Julia Breslin. Lanham, MD: Rowman & Littlefield Publishers.

Masriya, Aswat. 2014. "Egypt's Homosexuals Struggle for
    Freedom." *Egyptian Streets*. 8 April, 2014. Web.
    (Accessed: 29 March, 2015).
    <http://egyptianstreets.com/2014/04/08/egypts-
    homosexuals-struggle-for-freedom/>.

Mawjoudin. 2023. Web. (Accessed: 19 November 2023).
    <https://www.mawjoudin.org/audiovisual-campaigns>.

Mawjoudin We Exist. *Facebook*. Web. (Accessed: 19 November
    2023).
    <https://www.facebook.com/mawjoudin.tn/photos>.

McCarthy, John and Mayer Zald. 1977. "Resource Mobilization
    and Social Movements: A Partial Theory." *American
    Journal of Sociology* 82 (6): 1212-1241.

McCarthy, Justin. 2014. "Nearly 3 in 10 Worldwide See Their
    Areas as Good for Gays." *Gallup*. 27 August, 2014. Web.
    (Accessed: 20 March, 2015).
    <http://www.gallup.com/poll/175520/nearly-worldwide-
    areas-good-gays.aspx>.

McCombs, Maxwell. 2004. *Setting the Agenda: The Mass Media
    and Public Opinion*. Cambridge: Polity Press.

Media Matters for America. 2023. "Charlie Kirk says Chinese
    military installations are using TikTok to 'make our
    children more likely to be trans." *Media Matters for
    America*. 22 March 2023. Web. (Accessed: 14 November,
    2023).
    <https://www.mediamatters.org/charlie-kirk/charlie-kirk-
    says-chinese-military-installations-are-using-tiktok-make-
    our-children>.

Mekhennet, Souad, and Maïa de la Baume. 2011. "Moderate
    Islamist Party Winning Morocco Election." *New York*

Times. 26 November, 2011. Web. (Accessed: 7 May, 2015). <http://www.nytimes.com/2011/11/27/world/africa/moderate-islamist-party-winning-morocco-election.html?_r=0>.

Melucci, Alberto. 1996. *Challenging Codes: Collective Action in the Information Age*. New York: Cambridge University Press.

Merrill, Jamie. 2015. "Gay Rights Activists Defy Ugandan Laws by Publishing New LGBTI Magazine." 4 January, 2010. Web. (Accessed: 23 March, 2015). <http://www.independent.co.uk/news/media/press/gay-rights-activists-defy-ugandan-laws-by-publishing-new-lgbti-magazine-9955950.html>.

Miles, Matthew. 2013. "The Bully Pulpit and Media Coverage: Power Without Persuasion." *The International Journal of Press/Politics* 19 (1): 66-84.

Morgan, Joe. 2015. "Swedish Gay Man Jailed in Tunisia for 'Homosexual Acts'." *Gay Star News*. 8 February, 2015. Web. (Accessed: 25 March, 2015). <http://www.gaystarnews.com/article/swedish-gay-man-jailed-tunisia-homosexual-acts080215>.

Muhumuza, Rodney. 2014. "Uganda's Gay Community Celebrates Pride After Anti-LGBT Law Invalidated." *The Huffington Post*. 11 August, 2014. Web. (Accessed: 23 March, 2013). <http://www.huffingtonpost.com/2014/08/11/uganda-gay-pride-parade-_n_5668148.html>.

Mumtaz, Ghina, Nahla Hilmi, Willi McFarland, Rachel Kaplan, Francisca Ayodeji, Iris Semini, Gabriele Riedner, Oussama Tawil, David Wilson, and Laith Abu-Raddad. 2011. "Are HIV Epidemics Among Men Who Have Sex with Men

Emerging in the Middle East and North Africa?: A Systematic Review and Data Synthesis."*PLoS Medicine* 8 (8): 1-15.

Murphy, Timothy. 2005. "The Search For The Gay Gene.' *BMJ: British Medical Journal* 330 (7498): 1033.

Naar, Ismaeel. 2013. "Shifting Gear: Saudi Women Defy Driving Ban." *Al Jazeera*. 27 October, 2013. Web. (Accessed: 27 March, 2015). <http://www.aljazeera.com/indepth/features/2013/10/ shifting-gear-saudi-women-defy-driving-ban-2013102 7132853713829.html>.

Northam, Jackie and Halima Athumani. 2023. "A new anti-gay law in Uganda calls for life in prison for those who are convicted." *NPR*. 29 May 2023. Web. (Accessed: 19 November 2023). <https://www.npr.org/2023/05/29/1178718092/uganda-anti-gay-law>.

Oldershausen, Sasha. 2012. "Iran's Sex-Change Operations Provided Nearly Free-Of-Cost." 4 June, 2012. Web. (Accessed: 20 March, 2015). <http://www.huffingtonpost.com/2012/06/04/iran-sex-change-operation_n_1568604.html>.

Online Maps. 2012. "Africa Population Density." 23 September, 2013. Web. (Accessed: 7 May, 2015). <http://onlinemaps.blogspot.com/2012/09/africa-population-density.html>.

OpenNet Initiative. 2009a. "Algeria." Web. (Accessed: 8 May, 2015). <https://opennet.net/research/profiles/algeria>.

———. 2009b. "Morocco." Web. (Accessed: 8 May, 2015). <https://opennet.net/research/profiles/morocco>.

Outright International. "Iran." *Outright International*. Web. (Accessed: 15 November 2024). <https://outrightinternational.org/our-work/middle-east-and-north-africa/iran#:~:text=Iran%20allows %20transgender%20people%20who,LGBTIQ%2Drelated %20media%20and%20communications.>.

O'Riordan, Kate. 2012. "The Life of the Gay Gene: From Hypothetical Genetic Marker to Social Reality." *The Journal of Sex Research* 49 (4): 362-368.

Overseas Security Advisory Council. 2014. "Morocco 2014 Crime and Safety Report." United States. Department of State. Bureau of Diplomatic Security. 10 February, 2014. Web. (Accessed: 25 March, 2015). <https://www.osac.gov/Pages/ContentReportDetails .aspx?cid=15123>.

Palau, Anna and Ferran Davesa. 2013. "The Impact of Media Coverage of Corruption on Spanish Public Opinion." *Revista Española de Investigaciones Sociológicas* 144: 97-124.

Peace Insight. 2021. "Damj, Tunisian Association for Justice and Equality." *Peace Insight*. September 2021. Web. (Accessed: 18 November 2023). <https://www.peaceinsight.org/enorganisations/ damj/?location=tunisia&theme>.

Penketh, Anne. 2008. "Brutal land where homosexuality is punishable by death." The *Independent*. 6 March, 2008. Web. (Accessed: 26 March, 2014). <http://www.independent.co.uk/news/worldmiddle-east/brutal-land-where-homosexuality-ispunisha ble-by-death-792057.html>.

Pew Research Center. 2013. "The Global Divide on

Homosexuality: Greater Acceptance in More Secular and Affluent Countries." *Pew Research Center*. 4 June, 2013. Web. (Accessed: 20 March, 2015). <http://www.pewglobal.org/2013/06/04/the-global-divide-on-homosexuality/>.

———. 2022. "Americans' Complex Views on Gender Identity and Transgender Issues." *Pew Research Center*. 28 June 2022. Web. (Accessed: November 14, 2023). <https://www.pewresearch.org/social-trends/2022/06/28/americans-complex-views-on-gender-identity-and-transgender-issues/>.

Pfeiffer, Tom and Zakia Abdennebi. 2008. "Liberals and Islamists Clash Over Morocco 'Gay Wedding'." *Reuters*. 13 March, 2008. Web. (Accessed: 25 March, 2015). <http://uk.reuters.com/article/2008/03/13/uk-rights-morocco-idUKL0581448520080313>.

Pink News. 2007. "Home Office Loses Gay Algerian Deportation Case." 24 October, 2007. Web. (Accessed: 25 March, 2015). <http://www.pinknews.co.uk/2007/10/24/home-office-loses-gay-algerian-deportation-case/>.

Polity IV. 2010. "Polity IV Country Report 2010: Algeria." Web. (Accessed: 8 May, 2015). <http://www.systemicpeace.org/polity/Algeria2010.pdf>.

———. 2014a. "Authority Trends, 1962-2013: Algeria." Web. (Accessed: 26 March, 2015). <http://www.systemicpeace.org/polity/alg2.htm>.

———. 2014b. "Authority Trends, 1956-2013: Morocco." Web. (Accessed: 26 March, 2015). <http://www.systemicpeace.org/polity/mor2.htm>.

———. 2014c. "Authority Trends, 1959-2013: Tunisia." Web. (Accessed: 26 March, 2015). <http://www.systemicpeace.org/polity/tun2.htm>.

Putnam, Robert. 1988. "Diplomacy and Domestic Politics: The Logic of Two-Level Games." *International Organization* 42 (3): 427-460.

Ramdani, Nahila. 2011. "Algeria Tried to Block Internet and Facebook as Protest Mounted." 12 February, 2011. Web. (Accessed: 24 March, 2015). <http://www.telegraph.co.uk/news/worldnews/africaandindianocean/algeria/ 8320772/Algeria-tried-to-block-internet-and-Facebook-as-protest-mounted.html>.

Rawlinson, Kevin. 2014. "British Man Jailed for Four Months in Morocco 'For Being Gays'." *The Guardian*. 5 October, 2014. Web. (Accessed: 25 March, 2015). <http://www.theguardian.com/world/2014/oct/06/british-man-ray-cole-70-jailed-four-months-morocco-gay>.

Reger, Jo and Kimberly Dugan. 2001. "Exploring Social Movement Theories Through an Interactive Exercise." *Teaching Sociology* 29 (3): 332-342.

Rhanem, Karima. 2006. "Sex Scandal: Gay Porn Network Sentenced to 30 Years in Prison." *Morocco Times*. 6 March, 2006. Web. (Accessed: 25 March, 2015). <http://karimarhanem.skyrock.com/2167919511-Sex-Scandal-Gay-porn-network-sentenced-to-30-years-in-prison.html>.

Roberts, Matthew. 1995. "The Emergence of Gay Identity and Social Movements in Developing Countries: The AIDs Crisis as Catalyst." *Alternatives: Global, Local, Political* 20 (2): 243-248.

Roberts, Scott. 2015. "Morocco Jails 2 Men for Committing a 'Deviant Sexual Act'." *Pink News*. 5 March, 2015. Web. (Accessed: 25 March, 2015). <http://www.pinknews.co.uk/2015/03/05/morocco-jails-2-men-for-committing-a-deviant-sexual-act/>.

Salhi, Zahia. 2010. "Algerian Women, Citizenship, and the 'Family Code'." *Gender & Development* 11 (3): 27-35.

Schedler, Andreas. 2002. "The Menu of Manipulation." *Journal of Democracy* 13 (2): 36-50.

Schweiger, Laura. 2011. "EU Asylum Policy for Gays and Lesbians Criticized by LGBT Groups." *Deutsche Welle*. 19 May, 2011. Web. (Accessed: 25 March, 2015). <http://www.dw.de/eu-asylum-policy-for-gays-and-lesbians-criticized-by-lgbt-groups/a-15089739>.

Sheils, Conor. 2014. "Egypt's Gay Activists are Ready to Fightback." *Cairo Scene*. 28 September, 2014. Web. (Accessed: 29 March, 2015). <http://www.cairoscene.com/ViewArticle.aspx?AId=14210-Egypt's-Gay-Activists-Are-Ready-To-Fightback>.

Schumpeter, Joseph. 1950. *Capitalism, Socialism, and Democracy*. New York: Harper.

Sidiguitiebe, Christophe. 2014. "L'homosexualité au Maroc Devient-elle Moins Tabou?" *Telquel*. 16 May, 2014. Web. (Accessed: 25 March, 2015). <http://telquel.ma/2014/05/16/lhomosexualite-au-maroc-devient-elle-moins-tabou_136020>.

Sieczkowski, Cavan. 2014. "Sochi Mayor Says There Are No Gay People In His City." *The Huffington Post*. 27 January, 2014. Web. (Accessed: 26 March, 2014).

<http://www.huffingtonpost.com/2014/01/27/
sochi-mayor-no-gay-people_n_4673232.html>.

Similar Web. 2014. "Website Ranking: Top 50 Sites in Tunisia for
All Categories." Web. (Accessed: 8 May, 2015).
<http://www.similarweb.com/country/tunisia>.

Slimane. 2010. "Being Gay in Algeria Today." *Global Gayz*. 13
January, 2013. Web. (Accessed: 25 March, 2015).
<http://www.globalgayz.com/being-gay-in-algeria-today/
391/>.

Smith, David. 2010. "Gay Magazine Launched in Morocco." *The
Guardian*. 20 May, 2010. Web. (Accessed: 24 March,
2015).
<http://www.theguardian.com/world/2010/may/20/gay-
magazine-launch-morocco-rights>.

Stern, Jason. 2014. "Saudi Arabia Steps Up Censorship, Snaring
Activists." *The Huffington Post*. 27 May, 2014. Web.
(Accessed: 27 March, 2015).
<http://www.huffingtonpost.com/committee-to-protect-
journalists/saudi-arabia-steps-up-cen_b_5398145
.html>.

Stewart, Colin. 2018. "Rift splits Tunisian LGBT rights
advocates." *Erasing 76Crimes*. 25 April, 2018. Web.
(Accessed: April 1, 2024).
<https://76crimes.com/2018/04/25/rift-splits-tunisian-lgbt-
rights-advocates/>.

Sufian, Sandy. 2004. "HIV/AIDs in the Middle East and North
Africa: A Primer." *Middle East Report* (233): 6-9.

Tait, Robert. 2005. "A Fatwa for Freedom." *The Guardian*. 27
July, 2015. Web. (Accessed: 28 March, 2015).
<http://www.theguardian.com/world/2005/jul/27/
gayrights.iran>.

Tammen, Ronald, Jacek Kugler, Douglas Lemke, Allan Stam III, Carole Alsharabati, Mark Abdollahian, Brian Efird, and A.F.K. Organski. 2000. *Power Transitions: Strategies for the 21st Century*. Washington, D.C.: CQ Press.

Tarrow, Sidney. 2011. *Power in Movement: Social Movements and Contentious Politics*. New York, N.Y.: Cambridge University Press.

TGEU. 2012. "816 Reported Cases of Murdered Trans People Between January 2008 and December 2011." *Transgender Europe*. Web. (Accessed: 20 March, 2015). <http://www.transrespect-transphobia.org/uploads/images/maps/TvT-TMM-Map2008-11-en2.png>.

———. 2014a. "Legal and Social Mapping - World #1." *Transgender Europe*. Web. (Accessed: 20 March, 2015). <http://www.transrespect-transphobia.org/uploads/downloads/Legal-Social-Mapping2014/web_tvt_mapping_1_EN.pdf>.

———. 2014b. "Legal and Social Mapping - World #2." *Transgender Europe*. Web. (Accessed: 20 March, 2015). <http://www.transrespect-transphobia.org/uploads/downloads/Legal-Social-Mapping2014/web_tvt_mapping_2_EN.pdf>.

The Free Internet Project. "Laws to protect Internet Freedoms." Web. (Accessed: 12 January, 2024). <https://thefreeinternetproject.org/>.

Tierney, Dominic. 2016. "The Legacy of Obama's 'Worst Mistake'." *The Atlantic*. 15 April, 2016. Web. (Accessed: 14 November, 2023). <https://www.theatlantic.com/international/archive/2016/04/obamas-worst-mistake-libya/478461/>.

Tilly, Charles. 2004. *Social Movements, 1768-2004*. Boulder:

Paradigm Publishers.

Torbey, Carine. 2005. "Lebanon's Gays Struggle With Law." *BBC News*. 29 August, 2005. Web. (Accessed: 6 May, 2015). <http://news.bbc.co.uk/2/hi/middle_east4154664.stm>.

Tutton, Mark. 2010. "Algerian Transsexual's Memoirs Reveal Life of Discrimination." *CNN*. 9 July, 2010. Web. (Accessed: 25 March, 2015). <http://www.cnn.com/2010/WORLD/meast/07/09/randa.algeria.transsexual.lebanon/>.

UNHCR. 2007. "Algeria: Treatment of Homosexuals by Society and Government Authorities; Protection Available Including Recourse to the Law for   Homosexuals Who Have Been Subject to Ill-Treatment (2005-2007)." United Nations. United Nations High Commissioner for Refugees. 30 July, 2007. Web.   (Accessed: 25 March, 2015). <http://www.refworld.org/cgi-bin/texis/vtx/rwmain?page=country&category=&publisher=IRBC&type=&coi=DZA&rid=&docid=474e895c1e&skip=0>.

USA Today. 2019. "13 Countries where being gay is legally punishable by death." June 14, 2019. Web. (Accessed: March 26, 2024). <https://www.usatoday.com/picture-gallery/life/2019/06/13/iran-yemen-among-countries-where-being-gay-is-punishable-by-death/39574925/>.

U.S. Department of State. 2013. "Country Reports on Human Rights Practices for 2013: Morocco." United States. Department of State. Bureau of Democracy, Human Rights and Labor. Web. (Accessed: 25 March, 2015). <http://www.state.gov/j/drl/rls/hrrpthumanrightsreport/index.htm?year=2013&dlid=220369>.

———. 2016. "Tunisia 2016 Human Rights Report. United

States. Department of State. Bureau of Democracy, Human Rights and Labor. Web. (Accessed via The Wayback Machine: 19 November 2023).
<https://web.archive.org/web/20170307090415/https://www.state.gov/documents/organization/265734.pdf>.

———. 2022."2022 Country Reports on Human Rights Practices: Algeria." United States. Department of State. Bureau of Democracy, HumanRights, and Labor. Web. (Accessed: 12 January, 2024).
<https://www.state.gov/reports/2022-country-reports-on-human-rights-practices/algeria/>.

Wakefield, Lily. 2020. "Dozens of students handed prison sentences for the alleged 'crime' of attending a 'gay wedding'." *Pink News*. 16 October 2020. Web. (Accessed: 18 November 2023).
<https://www.thepinknews.com/2020/10/16/algeria-students-jail-for-attending-gay-wedding/>.

Watan, Cherfaoui. 2004. "Bouteflika Favorable à la Révision du Code de la Famille." *Algerie-DZ*. 11 October, 2004. Web. (Accessed: 24 March, 2015).
<http://www.algerie-dz.com/article1172.html>.

Weinthal, Benjamin. 2020. "Tunisia may have become first Arab country to recognize gay marriage." *The Jerusalem Post*. 29 April 2020. Web. (Accessed: November 15, 2023).
<https://www.jpost.com/middle-east/did-tunisia-just-become-first-arab-county-to-recognize-gay-marriage-626115#google_vignette>.

Whitaker, Brian. 2006. *Unspeakable Love: Gay and Lesbian Life in the Middle East*. Los Angeles, California: University of California Press.

Wong, Curtis. 2014. "Ricky Martin Changes 'She' To 'He' During

Performance Of 'She's All I Ever Had' In Morocco." *The Huffington Post*. 16 June, 2014. Web. (Accessed: 24 March, 2015). <http://www.huffingtonpost.com/2014/06/16/ricky-martin-pronoun-song_n_5499402.html>.

World Values Survey. 2010-2014. "Online Data Analysis." Web. (Accessed: 16 March, 2014). <http://www.worldvaluessurvey.org/WVSOnline.jsp>.

Yes People! We Do Exist! 2015. *Facebook*. Web. (Accessed: 28 March, 2015). <https://www.facebook.comIranianLGBTcommunity>.

Zarindast, Karen, and Saeedeh Hashemi. 2012. "Iran's Health Insurers to Pay for Sex Change Operations." *BBC News*. 29 May, 2012. Web. (Accessed: 28 March,   2015) <http://www.bbc.com/news/world-middle-east-18 258276>.